"This book is a wake-up call in all the how 'beauty' has been co-opted to bec for so many of us, distracting us from identity. In our image-based world, Me more important. We need this reminde soul-deep beauty."

Bob Goff, *New York Times* bestselling author

"Nothing is more shattered or misunderstood in our lives than beauty. We are unable on our own to recapture God's vision for it, and every generation needs guides who can reintroduce it to us again for the first time. In Melissa Johnson, we have such a guide, and with *Soul-Deep Beauty*, she has offered us a vision and a way not only to encounter, but to practice becoming the very beauty that God has foreseen us to be. Read this book, and find your soul's beauty emerging more truly than ever you imagined it could."

Curt Thompson, MD, author of *The Soul of Desire* and *The Soul of Shame*

"Every single day—maybe every single hour of most days—I talk about self-worth. I talk about identity and the way we see ourselves physically, emotionally, and spiritually. As a therapist for girls and families, one of my greatest hopes for every human who walks out of my office is that they would know their worth . . . inside and out. I'm so grateful for this book by Melissa Johnson that I believe can help them discover just that. *Soul-Deep Beauty* is what we all need in a world that is captivated by image and constantly pushing us toward perfection. There is so much more . . . to us and to the way God sees us. Thank you, Melissa, for pointing us toward true worth."

Sissy Goff, LPC, MHSP, bestselling author; speaker; and Director of Child and Adolescent Counseling at Daystar Counseling in Nashville, TN

"Melissa's message abruptly challenges society's tendency to make money off women's shame. She sheds light on the many lies that wreak havoc on women's hearts, minds, and bodies. Reading Melissa's words will call on the 'more' that your soul was made for. The truths in this book will allow you the grace, strength, and courage you so desperately need to fight off the shame and lies that you have been living in. I pray your heart be ready to receive, for there are many deep God truths wrapped in these pages."

Kathryn Shultis, Be a Blessing Co.

"This book will make you change your perspective from culture's standards to Christ's standards. The way Melissa captures the problem and solution to how we view beauty is absolutely necessary to understand."

Tori Hope Petersen, bestselling author of *Fostered*

"The best-kept secret of American culture is that it runs on shame, and we buy into it. Melissa Johnson exposes this reality with honesty and vulnerability, guiding readers to redefine beauty by developing a more soulful, holistic relationship with their bodies."

Steve Wiens, pastor and author

"With plenty of research and vulnerable storytelling, Melissa Johnson's book has the power to loosen the chains of shame and self-hatred that have been sold to women for generations. *Soul-Deep Beauty* will reorient readers to the Source of their true worth and help them counter cultural lies with the truth that they are whole, loved, and free."

Katelyn Beaty, editorial director of Brazos Press and author of *Celebrities for Jesus: How Personas, Platforms, and Profits Are Hurting the Church*

"An original contribution to the literature of beauty and body image from a Christian perspective. Johnson vividly demonstrates how the quest for physical perfection, as defined by our toxic culture, leaves us spiritually impoverished. One doesn't need to believe in God to appreciate her illuminating analysis and to applaud her recovery."

Jean Kilbourne EdD, award-winning filmmaker of *Killing Us Softly*

"Many of us know that we are swimming in toxic waters when it comes to issues surrounding body image, eating disorders, and our overall relationship to ourselves—which is why I'm deeply grateful for the resource that Melissa Johnson has provided us in her book *Soul-Deep Beauty*. With precision and compassion, Melissa helps name not only the wounds that plague us, but the source of hope and healing available to us as well. This is a sobering and yet hopeful book that is needed for such a time as this."

Aundi Kolber, MA, LPC, therapist and author of *Try Softer* and *Strong like Water*

"Melissa has a passionate heart for the true gift of God's beauty; one that frees, transforms, and heals. In this vulnerable, encouraging story, she invites her readers both to encounter that beauty and also to be defined by it rather than the false ideals of beauty so prevalent in the modern world. Her writing will be a gift to many."

Sarah Clarkson, author of *This Beautiful Truth: How God's Goodness Breaks Into Our Darkness*

"With both expertise and wisdom, Melissa Johnson gently guides readers through an honest examination of the distorted cultural norms we live in and ushers us into a thought-provoking consideration of true, soul-formative beauty. A timely and insightful read!"

Elizabeth Peterson, MA, CSD, spiritual director and retreat facilitator of Commune Soul Care

SOUL-DEEP
BEAUTY

SOUL-DEEP
BEAUTY

Fighting for Our True Worth in a World Demanding Flawless

MELISSA L. JOHNSON

BETHANYHOUSE
a division of Baker Publishing Group
Minneapolis, Minnesota

© 2023 by Melissa L. Johnson

Published by Bethany House Publishers
Minneapolis, Minnesota 55438
www.bethanyhouse.com

Bethany House Publishers is a division of
Baker Publishing Group, Grand Rapids, Michigan

Printed in the United States of America

Library of Congress Cataloging-in-Publication Control Number: 2022055256
ISBN 978-0-7642-4165-9 (paper)
ISBN 978-0-7642-4203-8 (casebound)
ISBN 978-1-4934-4247-8 (ebook)

Unless otherwise indicated, Scripture quotations are from THE HOLY BIBLE, NEW INTERNATIONAL VERSION®, NIV® Copyright © 1973, 1978, 1984, 2011 by Biblica, Inc.® Used by permission. All rights reserved worldwide.

Some names and recognizable details have been changed to protect the privacy of those who have shared their stories for this book.

The information in this book is intended solely as an educational resource, not a tool to be used for medical diagnosis or treatment. The information presented is in no way a substitute for consultation with a personal health care professional. Readers should consult their personal health care professional before adopting any of the suggestions in this book or drawing inferences from the text. The author and publisher specifically disclaim all responsibility for any liability, loss, or risk, personal or otherwise, which is incurred as a consequence, directly or indirectly, of the use of and/or application of any of the contents of this book.

Cover design by Faceout Studio

The author is represented by the literary agency of Pape Commons.

Baker Publishing Group publications use paper produced from sustainable forestry practices and post-consumer waste whenever possible.

23 24 25 26 27 28 29   7 6 5 4 3 2 1

CONTENTS

To Jared, my mom and dad, my sisters, my grandma Doris, and my aunt Karen. Thank you for showing me the heart of God through your understanding, love, care, and compassion. That is the greatest gift anyone can receive.

PART 1

A JOURNEY OF
RECOGNITION

1 THE RACE TO NOWHERE

Maybe you've been brainwashed too. —*The New Radicals*

I was thirty-one when I entered intensive eating disorder treatment and had the startling realization that I'd been brainwashed. I'd let the cultural idol of thinness deeply affect my sense of self, self-esteem, and aesthetic expectations, and only after about three months into that treatment did I start accepting my diagnosis and recognizing the major players in how my disorder came about.

While many factors contribute to the manufacturing of an eating disorder in someone's life, I've found none so unsettling and oppressive as the popular American discourse regarding women's body image.*

To say that culture caused my eating disorder would be an overstatement. But to say it didn't significantly affect my self-worth, self-expectations, and self-acceptance would be a gross understatement. I've realized that, while it may not be shouted from the rooftops, lurking beneath the New Year's resolution diets and Fitbit craze lies a

---

* Throughout my story, I often refer to "American beauty," as that is my cultural context. Though the beauty messages and cultural norms I discuss are prevalent in Western culture at large, I have simply experienced them in an American context.

13

sinister world of manipulation, judgment, prejudice, and marginalization. Our aesthetically obsessed culture has a disturbing underbelly.

With new eyes, I noticed how the media, advertising, and diet industries perpetually sell us on the idea that if we lose just a little more weight (or have just a few less wrinkles or "tone up" our bodies), we'll be happy. Perhaps you've noticed it too. And here's the clincher: We're buying it. *Literally.*

But what if we do lose the weight and are still no happier? Or what if because of our striving we're even more obsessed with food and our appearance? What if what we thought would bring us freedom and happiness does the opposite, further imprisoning us to cultural expectations? Believing in and following the rabbit trail of "never enough" messages is falling into a black hole. These messages are oh so nicely packaged, but the results they promise are also incredibly elusive. And if that's the rabbit trail we continue down, we eventually believe *we* will never be enough because what we *do* will never be enough.

Eating disorders, low self-esteem, anxiety, depression, self-harm, shame, body image struggles (body contempt, even), tumultuous relationships with food, jealousy and comparison among girls and women . . . This is just a sampling of the fallout I've seen in the wake of Western beauty culture. We're all swimming in the water of "never enough"—and it wears on us.

> We're all swimming in the water of "never enough"— and it wears on us.

In the pursuit of beauty and the elusive "beach-ready" body, women and young girls engage in all sorts of damaging, often overlooked practices, like restrictive eating, extreme or obsessive exercise, cosmetic surgery, and demeaning self-talk. These practices may be assumed or even blown off as the price to be beautiful or even to achieve wellness—a warped brand of both—but they take incredible energy of the mind and heart as well as a great deal of time. They have a dangerous gravity and can easily become a consuming force in our lives.

So as advertisers capitalize on our strivings and insecurities, I've been burdened by what's happening to the eternal and invaluable female soul as it bathes in the onslaught of "never enough."

Following the Rabbit Trail

Recently, I joined a couple dozen college-age women at a lovely retreat center in the Northwoods of Wisconsin. Towering pines, a picturesque chapel, the landscape bursting with green. There I was, a married woman and college professor, surrounded by these "girls" who were so full of energy, so full of dreams. As I watched and talked with them, I recognized the familiar striving for perfection. I saw myself in them. Wanting to do it all well—faith, family, friends, fitness, meaningful work—all while meeting the cultural standard for beauty.

They had so much to "perfect" in what they wore, what they ate, how they exercised. It felt exhausting to me, and my heart ached with compassion for them. They were simply following the script they'd been given. The script we've all been given.

From an early age, females learn the most acceptable way to be: kind, confident, and above all else, thin. Obviously, this expectation is rarely explained to us explicitly. As intuitive creatures, however, we learn it well. From cartoons to toys to movies, we assimilate what the ideal feminine body shape is: fit and thin. After all, what exemplary character in TV world doesn't adhere to that body type? From Barbie to Hannah Montana to Disney princesses, the message is communicated loud and clear: to matter, have value, and "be a main character," you must meet certain criteria.

Then as we grow up, we slowly learn the cold reality that the linchpin of that trifecta of kindness, confidence, and thinness is the aesthetic component. We may very well be kind and confident, but if we aren't thin, we're inconsistent with the cultural ideal. To matter, to have a voice, to be respected, we must achieve, maintain, or perfect a look. Thin, fit, and beautiful are supposedly our passport to cultural relevance.

As these same young girls grow up enduring the rigors of puberty and then young adulthood, media, advertisers, and diet culture are all glad to accompany them on that journey of maturation and development. Modern-day adolescents are rarely handed women who are, say, astronauts or aviators as cultural role models; rather, the heroes of today are celebrities whose greatest recent feat is losing ten pounds for swimsuit season. The artifacts that used to represent the path to adulthood have broadened from diaries and braces to scales and fitness apps. Such tools for self-assessment are steadily acquired, and the classic coming-of-age questions, *Am I smart enough?* and *Am I likable?*—in other words, *Am I good enough?*—are trumped by the paramount wondering, *Am I thin, fit, and pretty enough?* Essentially, *Am I culturally acceptable?*

> Thin, fit, and beautiful are supposedly our passport to cultural relevance.

As adult women, we discover the very same rules are at play. The messages are identical as we remain inundated with diet commercials and ads for the latest exercise equipment and all sorts of creams and contraptions to alter some body part that "needs" improvement. I imagine even the most confident of women find themselves considering what's wrong with how they are.

And just when we think we might be doing all right—in a healthy and balanced place with food, activity, and body image—some advertiser rolls out another ad about losing just a little more weight. After all, that woman looks dramatically less depressed after losing ten pounds, right?

I also started noticing how, in our culture, we marry weight loss with happiness, and we marry thinness with respect. Mentally scroll through the popular female news anchors, TV personalities, movie celebrities, and fitness and beauty influencers you know. Most are thin and fit, aren't they? And if they don't fit the cultural ideal, they're usually considered funny, and their appearance is to some extent a gimmick.

While that may not come as a huge surprise, reflect on what that communicates to us as women. Plainly stated, the females in our culture who have a voice and "matter" are largely thin. And in a media-saturated world, that reality has larger repercussions than may be assumed. With our society associating competency, respectability, self-discipline, beauty, health, and happiness with thinness, those who don't fit that cultural ideal are made to feel as though they don't measure up, they aren't good enough, they aren't as valued.

Furthermore, losing some weight, becoming more toned, or eating "cleaner" become the "obvious" conclusion for gaining any of the above—happiness, respectability, and all the rest. While some women may be immune to this cultural ideal, for many others, feeling inconsistent with the cultural norm can do severe damage to their self-esteem and, increasingly so, to their mental health.

Though all this may seem like feminist rhetoric, these realities have dire repercussions. One study showed that 97 percent of women have "at least one 'I hate my body' moment" in a day,[1] while another survey demonstrated that 75 percent of women between the ages of twenty-five and forty-five reported engaging in disordered eating.[2] We also know that "20 million women . . . will struggle with an eating disorder at some point in their lives."[3]

Please consider that those statistics represent *reported* occurrence of eating disorders or disordered eating, not necessarily women who are in denial or unaware of their eating struggles, as was the case in my own experience. Furthermore, eating disorders have the second highest mortality rate among all mental health disorders, surpassed only by opioid addiction.[4]

With teen depression, anxiety, and the occurrence of eating disorders on the rise, it's hard to believe that the prevailing thin ideal in the media isn't causing significant damage to the developing psyche, self-esteem, and soul of young women. As a therapist for adolescents, I've heard young girls despair over feeling as though they're not thin enough or pretty enough, and in intensive eating disorder treatment groups, I've heard grown women talk about how they're terrified to restore weight due to unhelpful comments people might make or, even worse, what they may say to themselves.

The truth is, we have a significant problem. We're actively equating women's worth with their appearance, and the ramifications are serious.

The question is, what are we going to do about it?

Back at the retreat, interacting with those college-age women, my compassion turned to alarm as conversations on the dock and in the chapel helped me see the depths to which the very same dangerous messages that had robbed me of so much are impacting this next generation. My mind flashed images of my youngest nieces, now only seven and five years old, and the pit in my stomach deepened.

> We're actively equating women's worth with their appearance, and the ramifications are serious.

I needed to do something. To say something. To sound the alarm.

Much like Alice in Wonderland, these beautiful young women were quickly scrambling after the elusive rabbit on that soul-sucking trail—the trail I was all too familiar with.

I wanted to warn them.

I want to warn you.

A Quest for More

This book tells the story of how I followed that rabbit trail and, as a result, seriously jacked up my life. I hope it will help you see that American beauty isn't beautiful at all; it's a race to nowhere. A race that's fracturing the minds, the relationships, and the very souls of women and girls in ways that are largely unnoticed.

The cultural water we're swimming in is toxic, but we aren't saying much about it. We've become so used to the water that we don't even notice it. Or if we do, we grossly underestimate its toxicity. For us. For our children.

Our bodies have become objects, commodities to be used for economic gain in the capitalistic rat race, leaving us broken. Our minds have become places to track calories and steps or to scrutinize our perceived flaws in allegiance to a diet, reset, or lifestyle that promises happiness. The rules and mantras of American beauty and diet culture have taken up residence in our internal scripts, impacting and infiltrating every aspect of our well-being. The broken kind of beauty we're being sold warps and fractures our souls on so many levels.

It's the ultimate deceit: as we chase after what promises to bring us acceptance and happiness, we're left only more broken. Disintegrated. Put another way, we're posting, filtering, and literally buying our own soul exploitation. Perhaps the worst part of all is that we don't realize we're being played. Advertisers and those in the beauty and diet industry are making billions off our shame—the very shame they purposely stir up.

> Advertisers and those in the beauty and diet industry are making billions off our shame—the very shame they purposely stir up.

But don't you believe you were made for more than running after aesthetic perfection amid the shame-filled "never enough"? An empty chasing of the wind—the elusive rabbit? Our eulogies can be a lot more meaningful than *She was so committed to eating clean*, or *She never missed a workout*, or *I think we can all learn from how flawless her body was*.

I believe we've all been created by a God of unending and unimaginable love. A God of adventure and creativity and wonder. A God of wild beauty. And I believe he has plans for your life, your heart, your mind, your activity in the world—for your true self to grow and thrive. And those plans have nothing to do with pursuing a warped brand of beauty or health. They don't last.

Are you weary of feeling like you don't meet the criteria for the "main character" aesthetic?

Are you exhausted by chasing trim and fit to prove your worth?

Do you experience an underlying anxiety about aging or keeping up (or even starting) a fitness routine?

Do you ever beat yourself up for not getting in enough steps or attaining or maintaining that New Year's resolution to lose weight?

Are you tired of the mental energy it takes to strive for attaining or maintaining perfect or clean nutrition?

Do you feel like no matter what you do, your body or your complexion or your whatever isn't flawless enough?

If so, I've got you. Take a deep breath, and please consider this an invitation to stop striving. In the pages ahead, I share so much I want you to know. You can choose something different from the shame-saturated, cultural beauty we've all been immersed in. Much more freedom is to be found. Thriving awaits you. And I believe that both individually and together we can shed the legacy of broken beauty and move into a different reality. One our souls are made for. We can choose that something different in our own lives, in our homes, in our friend groups. That's how culture changes. One person at a time.

Often what we know most acutely—the deep-in-your-bones kind of knowing—comes from well-worn and often difficult places along our journey. Sometimes to know something deep in your bones, you must experience it yourself. For me to see the dead end, ugliness, and fracturing that all lie in chasing after popular cultural beauty narratives, I had to get to the end of myself.

On the journey ahead, I'll show you how that fracturing occurred in my own life. But I'll also show you how the undoing of American beauty's effects opened me up to an entirely different kind of beauty. Sometimes the deconstruction of one thing leaves space for something far better, more beautiful, and real than the shaky thing there before. I want to show you how that new thing touches those soul-deep, longing places American beauty promises to fill but never can—and how that shift in how I know and understand beauty has made all the difference in the world.

Will you join me?

Are You Racing Too? A Self-Awareness Inventory

Honestly and thoughtfully complete the following inventory with simple yes or no answers to consider how cultural messages around beauty and body image may be impacting your relationship with food and your body. If you respond yes to any of the items below, consider if that tendency is affecting you in any negative, unhelpful way. Also consider whether you'd like to move toward greater freedom in that area.

- I often find myself fixated on my appearance.
- I often wish my body was thinner, smaller.
- I often wish I could change some things about my appearance.
- I often tailor my food choices to try to shrink or change my body.

- I often tailor my movement/exercise choices to try to shrink or change my body.
- I often feel preoccupied with thoughts about the size or shape of my body.
- I often feel preoccupied with thoughts or anxiety about what I will eat or what I've eaten.
- I often feel preoccupied with tracking steps, calories, or macros.
- I often find myself trying to "perfect" my food choices.
- I often compare my body to other women's bodies.
- I often compare my exercise routine to other women's routines.
- I often find myself judging other women's body shapes or sizes.
- I often label foods as good or bad.
- I would likely benefit from inviting more self-compassion into my relationship with my body.

A NOTE BEFORE THE JOURNEY AHEAD

Even if they haven't been diagnosed with an eating disorder or don't meet diagnostic criteria, anyone struggling with food, body image, or exercise can experience great distress and disorder in their life. And often people with eating disorders don't think they have one because they believe they don't look like they do. But eating disorders have no look. People of all shapes and sizes can have an eating disorder. Yet that myth about a look is too often a barrier to their seeking help. And, of course, anyone can have an eating disorder regardless of their gender, age, race, or ethnicity.

As you read my story or if in general you realize that your struggles with these topics bring marked distress or dysfunction into your life, please seek help. Obtaining an assessment from a therapist who specializes in eating disorders or from an eating disorder treatment program can be a valuable tool. An online assessment can be taken at https://www.emilyprogram.com/your-recovery/take-the-quiz/.

It can also be helpful to consider how much of your daily thought life is devoted to food, body shape and size, and exercise (10 percent, 80 percent, more?). Would you like to free up more head and heart space? My therapist once told me, "You could be more free." Is that true for you? If so, you can find resources and support from NEDA, the National Eating Disorders Association, https://www.nationaleating disorders.org/.

2 THE WRONG SIDE OF THE TABLE

The best way out is always through. —*Robert Frost*

It was all so surreal. In front of me, staring me down, sat that terrifying bratwurst. To my left sat my husband, Jared, and to my right was unfamiliar company.

It's not as if Jared and I had never eaten dinner together; we'd shared a meal hundreds of times, most often alone. This time, however, we were surrounded by not just other people, but virtual strangers. When we'd married three years earlier, I certainly hadn't envisioned having to be admitted to intensive eating disorder treatment. Moreover, I'd never envisioned the two of us eating a "therapeutic meal" together at Friends and Family Night. The fluorescent lights, Formica-topped tables, awkward small talk, and altogether sterile environment were all a far cry from our usual warmly lit dinners where intimate conversation and laughter flowed so naturally.

Now I was experiencing a mix of disbelief and embarrassment. The merging of my normal life and my life as a patient was suddenly overwhelming. I glanced across the table and looked at the program therapist, a woman I'll call Leah, who was intermittently introducing expected topics of small talk. I raised my gaze from the picnic fare on my plate to respond to her. There she sat—so put together. Her hair neatly tied back, her outfit so polished and fashionably preppy, and she always seemed so warm and approachable.

Then it hit me. I wanted to be Leah. In fact, I was used to being Leah, in a sense. She represented so much of what I wanted to emulate as a marriage and family therapist in my "normal life"—a kind and approachable young professional who just so happened to look very put together all the time.

I glanced at Jared, trying to tell if he noticed the similarities between Leah and me. I also examined his facial expressions and body posture. Was he embarrassed to be here with me? He'd married the Leah version of me, not whatever this was. My mind reeled as I tried to make progress on my now-cold bratwurst. *How did I get here?* I wondered. Weren't these glaring "self of the therapist" kinks supposed to be worked out in grad school? How did I miss this one? I wasn't supposed to be the patient. I wasn't supposed to be on this side of the table.

A Few Steps Back

So how on earth did I end up at Friends and Family Night that autumn evening with Jared? Months before, by all external appearances and cultural expectations, I seemed to have it all together. I was a young professional in my early thirties, married, with a recently purchased first home. My marriage was solid, I had some great friendships, and my house was usually pretty clean. I had worked hard to check all the boxes, and I think most people who didn't intimately know me at the time thought all was well. I had worked hard to do everything right, and if outward appearances were the measure, my efforts had paid off.

There was only one problem. No one had warned me about the downfalls of trying to be perfect. No one had explained how perfectionism can become an enemy.

At some point I'd bought the idea that I had to be perfect: engaging in purposeful work, being an always-there-for-you friend and family member, possessing a Pinterest-ready home and an Instagram-worthy marriage. And the cherry on top of all things perfect was my appearance. Not only did my hair have to be neat and styled and my outfit the perfect mix of preppy and trendy, but my body had to look a certain way too. I had to be fit, but not too fit, like I tried too hard. You know, like those J.Crew models who look effortlessly thin in their pressed business attire and perfectly carefree in their nautical-themed weekend wear.

> No one had explained how perfectionism can become an enemy.

Then at some point I was supposed to birth a child—or maybe several—before returning to my "save the world" career, once again donning my same-size, effortless J.Crew business suit.

In addition to being immersed in a culture that conveyed such expectations of perfection, I seemed to have the natural personality makeup to buy into cultural messages and expectations of me—hook, line, and sinker. Sensitive, perfectionistic, and a natural people pleaser, I wanted everyone to like me, I wanted to be all things to all people, and I wanted to look great while doing it.

Simple enough, right?

At some point all those self-imposed and cultural expectations hit a tipping point. Somehow all my perfectionistic energies got funneled into perfectionism around food, exercise, and body shape. What was once only one aspect of the collage of perfectionism became the be-all and end-all of my daily focus and the ultimate measure of my self-worth.

For years I'd participated in what I'd learned were "healthy" practices around eating and exercise. I'm by nature a rule follower, so when I was told to avoid certain foods, I certainly did. And when I was told to exercise regularly, I did that too.

If you're a rule follower like me, though, you know that too many rules suck the life out of you. As life anxieties increased, somehow a restrictive diet and a rigid exercise regimen became the primary outlets for that stress. And as I tried to manage my worry about stressors in my immediate family or my emotions about struggling clients, my repertoire of coping skills became increasingly myopic: the less food, the better (and it had to be "healthy" food), and the more exercise, the better. Sure, I could handle life in its vast array of stressors . . . as long as I could make it to the gym.

Finally, one day amid all the striving, I realized I couldn't do it all. I couldn't be the perfect wife, "save the world" worker, daughter, sister, friend, and homemaker. Furthermore, the obligatory standards for food and exercise I'd adopted as part of my daily routine had become exhausting. The rules I'd made a part of my life to attain the culturally ideal body image were taking so much time and energy, both physically and mentally. My list of acceptable foods was dwindling while my obligatory gym time steadily escalated.

Though I wouldn't have admitted it aloud, I knew I couldn't go on that way, and it felt like a colossal failure. I had given it my all. I had tried so hard to look good, eat well, work hard, do meaningful work, be kind and thoughtful . . . But the standards for perfection had evaded me. I'd failed.

So what did I do? I continued trying to look perfect, of course! I continued trying to play the part of the always-there-for-you friend and family member with the Pinterest-ready home and Instagram-worthy marriage—all while internally wondering, *Where do I go from here?*

The Invitation

Sometimes when we don't know what to do next, life itself invites us to take a pause. To step back, reassess, and redirect the momentum of our life. Though I now realized I couldn't perfectly meet all expectations and neatly check every box, I didn't know about the impending turn in the road that would speak to my *What now?* conundrum. As a failed perfectionist, I had no idea that my saving grace would come in the form of my therapist, Jane.

I'd been seeing Jane (not her real name) off and on for several years, sometimes regularly and sometimes on an as needed basis. Our relationship began almost a decade before I entered intensive eating disorder treatment. Most often we would talk about general anxieties, life's griefs and transitions, or the current relational struggles that week had brought. But from time to time, Jane broached the topic of my eating and exercise habits, and I easily brushed them aside as perhaps a bit rigid but easily within the normal range. After all, in my mind, many of my peers were also trying to eat healthily, and several of them had exercise routines just as strenuous as mine, if not more.

Plus, what woman didn't have my perspective on food and exercise? I thought. A chorus of articles, reports, and ads admonished us with all sorts of messages around diet and exercise. *More steps! Fewer carbs!* From my perspective, I was just following instructions.

We went on like this for years until, one day, Jane laid down the law during one of our regular Wednesday sessions, and I didn't see it coming. In her kind and gentle Jane way, she explained that she didn't think weekly outpatient therapy was effectively treating the severity of my symptoms.

Symptoms? Symptoms of what?

She went on to tell me about a couple of programming options I had for intensive eating disorder treatment.

Wait. Who called this an eating disorder?

Jane went on to explain the schedule for these programming options and the intake process. I'm pretty sure she could see my surprise and disbelief at what she was presenting. First, I didn't think I'd ever officially agreed that this whole eating and exercise situation was a disorder. And second, how did I get to the point of needing some sort of intensive treatment?

I told her I would think about it, and then I soberly exited our session, confused.

Weeks went by, and appointments with Jane came and went. Each time I entered our sessions, I anxiously wondered if she would revisit the treatment conversation, and then upon leaving, I breathed a sigh of relief because she hadn't pressed me to make a decision. On some level, it felt like one of those gunfights from old cowboy movies—who would draw first?

Well, I certainly didn't want to be the one to mention the massive elephant in the room. So for weeks and then months, I felt quite at ease, shrouded in my familiar defenses of avoidance and denial. I held them close like dear friends.

Until one day I realized avoidance and denial were not my friends at all.

Though I didn't mention the prospect of treatment in my sessions with Jane, I did mention the increasing distress I was experiencing. I felt like I was on a treadmill of self-imposed and cultural expectations. I kept trying to keep up, but the more I tried, the greater the treadmill's speed. Slowly, the ideals of eating healthily and being in shape turned into the dictatorial demand *You must be thinner.*

As the drive for thinness increased, my diet became increasingly restrictive, my fear of certain foods became greater, and my "need" to exercise in greater amounts spiraled. My nutrition waned, and my wellness diminished. The obsession with thinness ran rampant.

As the ante of those demands intensified, my desire for a solid marriage, good friendships, close family relationships, a meaningful career, and all the rest remained. The increasing rules around food and exercise made it all feel overwhelming and unsustainable. I felt like I was drowning as the voice of perfectionism made more demands, became less forgiving, and grew all-encompassing. I was completely exhausted.

Though I wanted anything but intensive treatment, my life had come to a sobering standstill. All the old answers, the old goals, were well worn and meaningless. In fact, my go-to scripts of perfectionism were not only not working, but were allowing self-judgment and despair to set up camp in my psyche.

> I felt like I was drowning as the voice of perfectionism made more demands, became less forgiving, and grew all-encompassing.

The only line I was being thrown in the midst of this standstill was Jane's offer of intensive treatment. So after thinking about it and fighting it, I finally surrendered to what I recognized as wisdom. I finally and exhaustedly decided to trust that Jane and the people who knew me best perceived something within me I didn't see: the source of my despair. I had adopted, internalized, and become overwhelmed with cultural expectations of beauty and performance and personal standards of perfection. So, with much hesitancy, I conceded to Jane's offer.

Something had taken hold of my life, and whether they called it an eating disorder or not, I had a problem and needed help.

Awakening

In one respect, this book is a personal narrative, the story of my journey in intensive treatment. In another sense, it's a story about waking up, about how I started to pay attention. What did I start paying attention to? So many things.

I began paying attention to my mind, my heart, and my intuition. I also started waking up to how the American culture I was immersed in assessed my value as a female. I began to see how certain body shapes are valued over others and how those deemed aesthetically pleasing are treated as though they're worth more. I awoke to how women are valued in America and in the world, and I didn't like it.

I also started to see the real-life implications of that value system. I noticed how it affected the women around me physically, mentally, and spiritually. How those cultural messages of worth don't remain cognitive abstractions but are adopted in women's minds and come to inhabit their souls.

Simply put, my eyes were opened to a new reality: Our aesthetically obsessed culture has significant casualties.

I invite you to be awakened to some of the same truths, observations, and even injustices I've come to know. I now see how what I once thought were independent realities are in fact inextricably connected and desperately in need of communicating with one another. Understanding the interrelatedness of Western standards of beauty, diet culture, disordered eating, shame, the soul, and God has in some ways saved my life and continues to do so. My hope is that you too will be awakened to these realities.

And may that awakening bring you life.

FOR REFLECTION

1. "I began to see how certain body shapes are valued over others and how those deemed aesthetically pleasing are treated as though they're worth more." Have you noticed this value

system for females? If so, how do you see it impacting girls and women?

_____

_____

_____

2. So often our high expectations for ourselves or perfectionism strengthen the voice of the inner critic. Do you notice that happening in an area of your life—perhaps somewhere you could invite in more balance or self-compassion? If so, what is that area? And how could you best issue that invitation?

_____

_____

_____

3 BROKEN BEAUTY

You can't get out of a cage you don't know you're in.
—*Greg Boyd, paraphrased*

For me, experiencing an eating disorder was like getting a PhD in social comparison. At some indefinable moment in my struggle, I reached an unfortunate tipping point. No longer did I assess my own worth by an internal measure based on my own values. Rather, my sense of self was dependent on external measures. I steadily became engrossed in this daily all-encompassing competition with those around me, with those in the media, and with myself. *Am I thinner than that person? Am I smaller than I was before? Is my portion of food smaller than theirs? Is my caloric intake less than yesterday's?*

If you ran, I wanted to run farther. If you went to the gym, I wanted to work out longer than you had—and longer than I had the previous week. It was a fierce game of social comparison with others and comparison with myself, and the rules were simple: eat even less food and do even more exercise. In this game, the ante was always upped, and the new norm was never enough.

Becoming addicted to comparison was certainly never anything I set out to do intentionally. Nor was this comparison process ever helpful or result in feelings of contentment. It was a tendency that gained significant momentum suddenly and usually ended in some sort of self-deprecation.

Because I knew the internal battle of social comparison associated with an eating disorder, in intensive treatment I soon learned that entering a new group was not for the faint of heart. My first day was even worse than entering a new level of treatment.

There I stood, equal parts terrified and awkward, with all sorts of thoughts racing through my head. *Why am I here, again? Do I really need to be here? What will these people think of me? Is an eating disorder even a real thing? What kind of person has an eating disorder? Even worse, what kind of person has an eating disorder in their thirties?*

My anxiety reached new heights as the door to the group room came into view, and only thanks to autopilot did I take my first steps inside. Whoever designed those group rooms must have anticipated the angst I would be feeling that day. They seemed to have done everything in their power to make this unsettling environment soothing, neutral, and all the things a group therapy room probably should be.

But despite the earth-toned furniture, nature-themed and inspirational art, and faux living room setup, I remained unnerved. As I felt the weight of eyes on me, I imagined all the judging, assessing, and sizing up the group members were doing as they watched the new girl enter the room and make her way to its safest-looking corner.

Maybe these women weren't judging me, at least to that extent, but I assumed they, like me, had spent ample time developing an inner critic toward all things aesthetic. I projected all of my own self-judgments and personal aesthetic critiques onto them. I imagined all of these assessments being hurled onto me, piling up, as I entered that room. It felt heavy.

Years later, I now see that those judgments and critiques were likely of my own making. Harsh assessments from the vaults of my own mind. However, after many more days of programming and conversations in group rooms just like that one, I learned I was largely right about one aspect—the inner critic part. These brave, kind, thoughtful, and loving women from all walks of life (and with so much beauty in them) heard the same all-too-common oppressive taunt I heard— *You'll never be good enough.*

You see, the eating disorder has this voracious energy for raising the bar. There's always more weight to be lost, more food to be restricted or "perfected," or more time to be spent working out. It always begs for just a little bit more and has a tremendous knack for making what *is* not good enough. It has a talent for whispering a new goal of perfection, and once that goal is fought for and reached, it informs you there's now a new goal. Contentment, gratitude, or self-congratulation are all in opposition to upping the goals of the eating disorder, because without the internal tyrant voice that always demands more of you, perfection is unattainable.

Essentially, perfection is a moving target. There's always some new goal to reach and more striving to do. And someone is always better than you are.

About six months into intensive treatment, it finally struck me that so much of the elusive promises of the eating disorder had been adopted from the American culture I was immersed in—those toxic waters I've mentioned. And the same "never enough" messaging of the disorder is mimicked in media, social media, advertising, and the diet industry. I recognized a surprising parallel process present in both American culture and in the thought life of many who suffer from eating disorders. It was striking and unnerving.

I became angry as well. My trying to do it "right" by cultural terms had only pulled me deeper into the hole of disorder and obsession. And suddenly it seemed so cruel. As women have become increasingly valued for their thinness culturally, the female psyche seems to have picked up on it. Consequently, happiness and societal acceptance seem to be an intuitive outcome of losing just a little more or a lot more weight. Have you noticed it too?

I also realized I'd internalized the demands of American media and the diet industry and made it my own personal value system. But the glaring problem is that this value system is a slippery slope, a burdensome tyrant with endless demands.

In very technical terms, I realized it's a life suck.

Selling Perfection

As it turns out, I'd not been alone in my pursuit of this elusive perfection and my dissatisfaction with "what is." In fact, due to the pervasiveness of body dissatisfaction, the *Oxford Handbook of the Psychology of Appearance* has labeled this phenomenon "normative discontent."[1] Essentially, so many people are discontent with their bodies that it's now considered part of the normalized human experience. The documentary *The Illusionists* even says the pursuit of the perfect body has become so prevalent that "it has become our new religion."[2]

The phenomenon of dissatisfaction with our bodies is especially notable among females, and it starts young. Research has demonstrated that girls as young as six years old desire to be slimmer.[3] And one in four children "have engaged in some kind of dieting behavior" by the time they're seven years old.[4]

> The phenomenon of dissatisfaction with our bodies is especially notable among females, and it starts young.

Additionally, in one study, 91 percent of the college-aged women surveyed "admitted to controlling their weight through dieting."[5] And in research among this same age group, "54 percent stated they would rather be run over by a truck than be fat," and "two-thirds said they would rather be mean or stupid than fat."[6]

Two themes are clear: (1) body dissatisfaction among women is epidemic, and (2) our society values thinness, apparently more than life itself for some. So how on earth did we get here? How did we as women become so dissatisfied with our bodies, and how did the pursuit of thinness become such a high-stakes game? I believe the answer lies at an interesting cross section of certain sociocultural trends and phenomena.

For one, researchers have noted the effect advertising has on popular trends and beliefs within a culture. Activist and writer Jean Kilbourne discusses how advertising not only sells products but sells "values, images, and concepts of . . . normalcy."[7] The idealized image and lifestyle portrayed in advertising "tells us who we are and who we want to be."[8] American advertising, then, plays a significant role in setting standards for beauty, desirability, who we think we *should* be, and how we think we *should* look. What American advertisements *don't* portray perfectly appointed, post-HGTV transformation homes; perfectly groomed children; bright and shiny automobiles; trim waists; and attractive fashions? Virtually none.

Advertising shapes culture because it portrays the cultural ideal to strive for. Laced within this idealized portrayal of American life is the assumption that attaining these glorified standards will result in happiness and acceptance. And it's also not-too-subtly implied that the products featured in these ads will help you attain all facets of this happiness-saturated, idealized American lifestyle.

Such dynamics of American advertising are more significant when considering Americans' daily inundation of advertisements. The marketing firm Yankelovich, Inc., estimated that a person living in a city is exposed to five thousand advertisements a day,[9] and the documentary *The Illusionists* states that we're at the point of media saturation, spending more than 80 percent of our waking hours exposed to some sort of media.[10] Essentially, Americans are continually flooded with both conscious and subconscious messages about idealized images and lifestyles every day—again, telling us who we *should* be and what we *should* look like.

How can we help but be influenced by such prescriptive persuasions? As *The Illusionists* states, "Flawless beauty is on display everywhere: in street ads, newspapers, magazines, TV, films . . . as well as in video games and pornography. The very quantity of these images makes it impossible for people not to be affected by them."[11] Advertising executives are literally banking on the fact that we *are* affected by them.

Such idealized images in American advertising are so crucial to consider because "should" has power. Social comparison theory teaches us about the human tendency to compare ourselves with others.[12] As social beings, we tend to gauge our own self-assessment or self-esteem by how we compare to others. Ads (including product endorsements by social media influencers) featuring people who seem to have reached physical perfection set the bar for what's considered ideal or normal in a society, and then the natural human tendency is to compare ourselves to that social ideal or indicated norm.

By using such idealized, "perfect" models, advertisers "can be seen as actively promoting a self-improvement motivation for comparison."[13] And this tendency is in fact very convenient for the beauty and diet industries trying to sell us products. For we know the "ideal consumer is someone who is anxious, depressed and constantly dissatisfied," and "academic studies from the most respected institutions show that sad people are bigger spenders."[14]

And so we see this is all very much on purpose.

Unkind.

Even cruel.

Our society also breeds this sort of social comparison by publishing magazine segments like "Who Wore It Better?" So the developing and impressionable minds of preteen, adolescent, and adult Americans are spending time and energy thoughtfully analyzing who looks better in some dress? And we're invited to this comparative exercise each month as a new issue arrives in our inbox.

I can only imagine how we then universalize that same process of analyzation among our female counterparts: *Do I look better in this dress, or does that woman look better in hers? Is my body more attractive than my friend's body? How do my abs compare to that Instagram influencer's?* The female psyche has been inundated with a warped social pecking order, and then in subtle and not-so-subtle ways we're encouraged to apply that lens to how we observe ourselves and other women.

The Incredible Shrinking Woman

The promotion of social comparison in American culture is unfortunate, because the thin female ideal portrayed in the media and advertising is not the norm at all. One study showed that the typical model was 20 percent underweight, meaning they met a diagnostic criterion for anorexia nervosa and then some (being 15 percent underweight was one of the diagnostic criteria for anorexia in the Diagnostic and Statistical Manual of Mental Disorders, or DSM-IV).[15] In fact, the thin ideal generally portrayed in advertising and the media is "possessed naturally by only 5% of American females."[16]

Also, as a whole, the historical trajectory of the norm for women in media and advertising has become progressively thinner. From the more voluptuous-figured Marilyn Monroe of the 1950s to the "heroin-chic" Kate Moss of the 1990s to the often emaciated models of the 2000s, the aspirational ideal body has become increasingly thinner.[17] In more recent years, the trend of "thin and toned" has gained popularity, as has the slim-thick trend popularized by influencers (think Kim Kardashian). A slim-thick figure is described as "a woman with a small waist, flat stomach and larger hips, bum and thighs, who is toned or considered physically fit."[18]

While some believed this trend to be a helpful shift from the waifish-thin ideal, a recent study showed that participants who were exposed to the slim-thick imagery experienced more weight and appearance dissatisfaction and diminished body satisfaction than those exposed to the thin ideal in the study.[19] One proposed theory as to why: because this ideal isn't any more obtainable than the thin ideal we might be more used to. The study noted that this body type can be achieved only through plastic surgeries or extreme, focused workouts.

All of that to say, I wouldn't suggest that the thin ideal or "fit and thin" ideal has lost momentum. But I would say another unrealistic or often unhealthily attained option has been added to the mix.

As women, we learn that to attain or embody the cultural ideal is to have social capital, to be valued in our culture for reflecting what's considered beautiful. You have arrived, in a sense, if you embody what our culture deems desirable. And as if the "ideal" body weren't hard enough to chase after, the standard for aesthetic "perfection" has gained new momentum with developing technologies.

Jean Kilbourne describes how today's aesthetic ideal for women is based on "absolute flawlessness,"[20] and thanks to photo airbrushing and computer retouching, blemishes and wrinkles are removed and bodies are edited to often anatomically impossible proportions. In fact, "The supermodel Cindy Crawford once said, 'I wish I looked like Cindy Crawford.'"[21]

Unfortunately, we see such slim, toned, "flawless" images in media and advertising and then try to reflect that same image back to the world in our social media accounts, often using apps or filters to "perfect" our image. Research shows that almost two-thirds of American adults "who have shared their photo online (64%) admit to having edited one prior to posting it,"[22] and in one survey "80 percent of girls said they had already applied a filter or used a retouching app to change the way they look in their photos by age 13."[23]

The fact that the images of women "portrayed by the media are rarely real"[24] has resulted in largely unrealistic, often contradictory (rail-thin, large-breasted) portrayals of the female body. Even though the idealized female form in American culture is unnatural on a number of levels, the frequency with which American women are exposed to the "slender, full-breasted, and well-toned"[25] ideal leads them to believe that's what a normal female can and should look like. This additionally leads women to believe "that [the thin ideal] is possible [with] enough effort and self-sacrifice."[26]

So here we are as a society, drowning the developing neural networks of young girls and the sacred minds of female adults with an ideal for comparison that's unrealistic, frequently literally unreal, and often associated with disordered or even pathological beliefs and behaviors. Advertisers, well-versed in the ways of human nature, know very well that women will compare themselves to that cultural standard. It could be said that continuing to dole out this sort of unrealistic cultural ideal for beauty is irresponsible, even dangerous.

In so many conscious and subconscious ways, our society is communicating to females that their appearance, the embodied self they present to the world, is not good enough, that they're missing the mark for what's considered ideal. And then we sit back in stupefied wonder, asking ourselves why so many young people are struggling with low self-esteem and body image these days.

The impact of these idealized images is profound. For one, women's body dissatisfaction and dissatisfaction with overall appearance increases after exposure to media images of thin women versus more average-sized women.[27] And body dissatisfaction has been found to be a central risk factor in developing low self-esteem, depressive mood, anxiety, and eating disorders,[28] while negative body image among adolescents has been correlated with depression, anxiety, and suicidality.[29]

Feel free to take a deep breath. This is a lot of heavy information. I get it. And if you personally struggle or someone close to you struggles with comparison or body image, this can be a lot to take in. But while all this is overwhelming, my aim is that waking up to these sobering realities moves us toward something different.

Long story short, as Jean Kilbourne says, these "images of idealized, unattainable beauty . . . that [do] not really exist in nature and that can be obtained only through cosmetic surgery . . . or digital retouching" are impacting us. They're impacting the upcoming generation. In so many ways. Kilbourne goes as far as to say, "The obsession with thinness is a public health problem."[30]

Diet Culture

Have you ever had one of those moments when "the lights turn on," so to speak? As in you've been experiencing something you haven't been able to define but then suddenly someone puts words to it for you? There's a normalizing and a settling in the naming. Like, *I'm not the only one who's been feeling this.* Naming things somehow makes them more manageable. It also helps us move toward change. How can we change something we don't put a definition around or understand?

For me, that was the case with registered dietitian and author Christy Harrison. I interviewed her for the *Impossible Beauty* podcast, and since "Hi. You need to know you changed my life" seemed like an overwhelming greeting, I just went with "Welcome to the podcast." But it's true. (Thanks, Christy. You did change my life.)

The change began when Christy introduced me to "diet culture" via her popular *Food Psych* podcast. It pulled off the blinders in so many ways, and I started seeing diet culture and its impact *everywhere.*

This is how Christy defines diet culture:

Diet culture is a system of beliefs that equates thinness, muscularity, and particular body shapes with health and moral virtue;

44

promotes weight loss and body reshaping as a means of attaining higher status; demonizes certain foods and food groups while elevating others; and oppresses people who don't match its supposed picture of "health."[31]

Put another way, particular body shapes (largely the thin and toned type) are equated with being healthy and virtuous. Additionally, changing our weight and our bodies has been sold to us as the silver bullet to the good life, the way to increase our health, general goodness, and social status.

Christy and a growing number of dietitians are in fact calling themselves "anti-diet dietitians," meaning that they will not recommend intentional weight loss for clients, and that health comes in all kinds of body shapes and sizes. Christy and her counterparts are anti-diet culture because of how pursuing diets and the thin ideal steals our money, time, and energy.

I'll add that chasing after the thin ideal can deplete the soul—the essence of who we are. Our soul is impacted by the multifaceted layers of our selfhood: our thought life, our emotions, our embodied experience, our sense of meaning and purpose, and our connection with others and with God.[32] Chasing after broken beauty can impact all of that, and we'll talk more about this in a later chapter.

To make this increasingly confusing and nefarious at the same time, as Christy puts it, "By and large, Western culture is diet culture."[33] The way Western culture has taught us to think about food and our bodies is so in the water we swim in that, again, we barely notice it. And as in my case and many others', these days diet culture is showing up less as an explicit "diet" (largely because research has shown traditional diets to be ineffective, with anywhere between 90 and 98 percent of weight-loss program participants regaining the weight they lost[34]) and more so under the guise of "health, wellness, and fitness."[35] In fact, the term *orthorexia*, which refers to the obsession with eating healthily, is an emerging category in the field of eating disorders.[36]

So whether it's a traditional diet program (like Jenny Craig or Weight Watchers) or a diet/diet culture rearing its head under the guise of a "lifestyle change," "a cleanse," or a "reset," "restricting calories and/or food groups is likely to disrupt someone's relationship with eating. In most cases, dieting (by any name) can lead to fixation and bingeing."[37]

So let's break this down a bit. Practically speaking, diet culture shows up when you're served dessert and your uncle says with a mix of charm and disapproval, "A moment on the lips, a lifetime on the hips." Or your friend talks about how guilty she feels for eating x, y, or z. It's when we label foods as good or bad, count calories or macros, or become fixated on the number of steps on our Fitbit or how "clean" our food is. It's when we assume someone's health by the size or shape of their body. It's when certain bodies are given more social status and more respect. It's when "health and wellness" is synonymous with "thin and toned" and we're told in subtle and not-so-subtle ways to chase after it.

Sadly, the obsession with thinness and equating thinness with health and morality, as Harrison puts it, has led and is leading to all kinds of disordered relationships with food, including dieting, diagnosable eating disorders, and disordered eating, which includes "fasting, chronic restrained eating, restricting major food groups, vomiting, or [using] laxatives to try to lose weight, and/or bingeing, as many people do as a result of dieting."[38]

All this to say the internalized motto of an eating disorder—"thinner is better"—has progressively been amplified in popular culture as the American ideal for health and morality as well as the American ideal for beauty. The voice of the eating disorder and the voice of our culture sing in unison. This is powerful, loud, and decidedly hard to drown out. And diet culture's "thinner is better" refrain is not only impacting women and girls' relationships with their bodies and food but with every facet of their well-being.

Shame Sells

This shapeshifting from the traditional old-school "diet" to the new "health and wellness" rebrand makes all the sense in the world when considering profits. According to the research firm Marketdata, the diet industry is profoundly lucrative to the tune of $72.6 billion.[39] And if we include the worldwide market for "healthy eating, nutrition, and weight loss," the profits jump to $648 billion.[40] Furthermore, a striking 85 percent of customers purchasing weight-loss products and services are women.[41]

Such statistics should leave us reeling. Clearly, the diet (and wellness) industry is affecting the women of America, or we wouldn't be spending so much money trying to change ourselves. Despite the false promises laced in our daily inundation of blaring diet-related commercials, infomercials, billboards, magazines, and online ads, we seem to be buying into these advertisements' implied message: *You're not quite good enough the way you are.*

I would argue that one of the most pervasive and malicious messages of an eating disorder and in American consumerist diet culture is one and the same: *No matter what you do, it will never be good enough. The bar will consistently be raised.* In either case, there's always one more product to buy or one more pound to lose.

Some researchers argue that this is exactly the game advertisers are knowingly trying to win. If women are given unattainable aesthetic norms and continually inundated by messages of who they should be and what they should look like, advertisers are guaranteed continued product consumption. Paul Hamburg, assistant professor of psychiatry at Harvard Medical School, puts it this way: "The media markets desire. And by reproducing ideals that are absurdly out of line with what real bodies really do look like . . . the media perpetuates a market for frustration and disappointment. Its customers will never disappear."[42] So while we're bending over backwards doing the latest "cleanse" or buying the newest abs contraption, we're seemingly unaware of our own exploitation.

In usual fashion, the worldly perpetual pursuit for money and power results in the marginalization of certain populations, and in the multibillion-dollar dieting industry, that marginalized population is women. If advertisers can continue to convince us we're never quite thin enough, youthful-looking enough, or close enough to the evolving cultural ideal, their profits will no doubt continue as well.

I only wonder if we as women will stay convinced.

The Commodification of the Female Body

Our pocketbooks are not the only thing being used. The female body itself has become a means to an end. Our bodies have become pawns in the buying and selling of goods in America. They've become something to assess, challenge, improve upon, and tweak. Our value is in our beauty, in our thinness, and so we're taught to use our money to improve our primary asset, our external aesthetic. Our bodies have somehow become divorced from our souls. Instead of being valued for our humanity, our worth is rated by our external appeal and how closely we match the cultural ideal. Our bodies have become objects, commodities to be used for economic gain in the capitalistic rat race.

As someone who believes in the infinite value of all humans, for me, the commodification of the female body has been extremely disturbing to assimilate. I can't begin to imagine the depths to which God is mourning all this. Reducing sacred beings made of body, mind, and spirit to an objectified tool for others' economic gain is not just disturbing but dehumanizing. When someone becomes an object rather than a living, breathing sacred being, all sorts of havoc unfolds.

The world is full of broken systems that dehumanize the human soul for the sake of the almighty dollar. You see it not just in advertising, where sex sells, but also in the pornography industry and the paramountly tragic sex trade. When we stop seeing a person as infinitely valuable, heinous things can be justified. In all these instances, the female body is reduced to a means for another's pleasure or economic gain.

I've been saddened and shocked to see how the diet industry and the media's exaltation of a narrow aesthetic ideal can be added to the list of systems that dehumanize. Amid the flurry and greed of the diet industry and the commodification of the female body in the media, an entirely unique and twisted value system has been created. The diet industry, pornography industry, and any other media venue that pivots on the maxim that "sex sells" depends on upholding and projecting the thin ideal. What sells is valued. And "fit and sexy" sell.

So beware. You are being sold a package of goods that banks on the fact that American women will want to keep up with the Joneses. This time, however, the Joneses are fit, toned, and always bikini ready.

In all this, I realized how I had underestimated the black hole that is the human striving for power and money. Sadly, we are capable of reducing others' humanity to elevate ourselves. And apparently it's quite advantageous for the powers that be in advertising to convince American girls, adolescents, and women that what is, is not good enough. Our bodies can always be leaner, our muscles more toned, our faces less wrinkled. Again, the advertising industry is banking on the fact that we're affected by them—and on our consumeristic drive to never be satisfied with how we are.

The Fallout

So what does all this mean for us women, we who are holistic beings, whose souls are not in fact divorced from our bodies? What happens to the human soul when it's inundated daily with the message that what is, is not good enough and we are led to compare ourselves so often to unrealistic ideals?

Renowned shame researcher Brené Brown defines shame in the following way: "The intensely painful feeling or experience of believing that we are flawed and therefore unworthy of love and belonging."[43] According to this definition, the media and advertising industries are shame-saturated systems, constantly communicating that we are indeed flawed and we can always work at more closely aligning with the flawless images on our television screens and social media feeds, in our magazines, and in our favorite movies.

Anxiety and shame work in tandem in American advertising. We are constantly being convinced that we aren't doing it right, we really should be doing it right, and there's a product to make sure we do it right. We're continually encouraged to strive to do better, eat better, exercise more, take the right supplements, do the right cleanse—to compare ourselves to whatever they say we can achieve. This unquiet energy to continue to strive is the lifeblood of consumerism. And even on the rare occasion that our body and skin are currently culturally acceptable, advertising executives can always bank on the fact that we're getting older and gravity will take its toll.

> While advertisers are capitalizing on our strivings and insecurities, what is happening to the eternal and invaluable female soul?

I recently came across this statement: "Anxiety is highly profitable."[44] And I'm realizing all the time how true that is. While sex sells, in a sad and ironic twist, it seems that shame and anxiety also sell.

Again, I only wonder about the fallout for those of us who are on the receiving end of these messages. While advertisers are capitalizing on our strivings and insecurities, what is happening to the eternal and invaluable female soul?

A Moving Target

As you can see, caught up in the mix of media saturation, diet culture, and photoshopped and filtered images, being a female in Western culture is not for the faint of heart. So many girls and women are internally beating themselves up, wearying their psyche and soul as they seek to attain the elusive goal of looking perfect.

Not only do media, diet culture, and advertising hand women this flawless body standard, but they also kindly sell us the means to seek after that standard via the latest cleanse, miracle diet pill, exercise plan, fitness app, or gym membership. One author discusses how increasing numbers of college women deemed "otherwise psychologically normal" are growing more and more consumed with dieting, restricting calories, and rigorous exercise as they pursue this ideal.[45]

In the fury of these feverish efforts, we must ask ourselves if we truly believe we will arrive at aesthetic perfection. Is there a foreseeable endpoint in all this striving? Will we ever be satisfied with "what is" rather than comparing ourselves to what someone else says we should be? I imagine not.

The restless energies of perfectionism, eating disorders, disordered eating, and consumerist culture all hinge on our unceasing discontent with "what is." Seeking to attain the American ideal for beauty is seeking to attain what's inherently elusive. Perfection is a moving target with a ravenous craving for better, thinner, and more.

And because perfection is never satisfied, this pursuit can craftily and steadily become an all-consuming endeavor. In my own life, I've observed how the thin ideal can subtly and progressively pervert good and natural desires—how the desire to be a good steward of one's body and eat healthily can easily progress to food restriction and self-deprivation. How the drive to be physically healthy can transform physical activity into an obsession or an exercise of self-contempt or even self-punishment. What begins with good intentions can gradually and stealthily progress into compulsive or restrictive thoughts and behavior as the demands of perfection gain momentum. Perfection becomes a taskmaster that depletes life versus the false end goal that promised to give life.

On a deeper level, we must ask ourselves if meeting the cultural ideal for beauty brings us deep joy and relational intimacy, what I believe we truly long for.

Research and my experience tell me no. Therapist, author, embodiment researcher, and another hero of mine, Dr. Hillary McBride, says it this way: "All of the empirical research tells us that we don't actually become happier when we change our bodies to meet appearance ideals."[46] Instead, we see peoples' compulsion around exercise increase, as well as anxiety about weight and their body, and their sense of conditional belonging increases the closer their body gets to the appearance ideal. Dr. McBride goes on to state, "It doesn't matter if you keep trying to change your body. If that's the way you're trying to feel OK, not only will you not feel OK, [but] you'll probably feel worse . . . that's where the real work is . . . in learning to be OK with ourselves as we are."[47]

I've witnessed how the tempting whispers that say losing just a little more weight or being a bit more toned will bring about happiness, deep contentment, or unanimous social acceptance are a fallacy. Societal voices promise what they cannot deliver. The obsession with comparison and the pursuit of perfection never brings joy or relational intimacy. They run counter to those true longings of the soul.

If you're seeking happiness and fulfillment by attaining the cultural ideal, your striving will never be enough to satisfy perfection. I guarantee it. This is not meant as a discouragement but rather a statement about the nature of perfection. Again, perfection is a moving target.

I invite you to imagine, as I believe, that women have been created for much more than this lifeless striving, this tiresome comparison, this exhausting race that leads to nowhere. Consider that the games of comparison, perfectionism, and consumerism are distracting us from what's truly worth our time.

> Obsession with comparison and the pursuit of perfection never brings joy or relational intimacy . . . those true longings of the soul.

FOR REFLECTION

1. Where and how are you seeing perfection sold these days (social media, media, advertising)? What emotions come up for you when you encounter these messages and images?

2. "Shame sells." Have you found this to be true? How does this statement strike you?

3. Media literacy is "the ability or skills to critically analyze for accuracy, credibility, or evidence of bias the content created and consumed in various media, including radio and television, the internet, and social media."[48] In other words, practicing media literacy is thoughtfully assessing media, often for its persuasion. When viewing media, social media, or advertising, helpful questions might be:

- Is someone trying to sell me something?
- What is the implied message here, or what is the implied message someone is trying to convince me of? (If you buy *x*, you'll be happy or more socially acceptable.)
- Is this image real? What's been retouched? What body parts have been dramatically reduced or enhanced?
- How might media literacy help disarm cultural messaging around beauty and thinness?

FOR FURTHER STUDY

- Watch a prime example of media literacy in this lecture by Jean Kilbourne (suggested clip: 0:00-7:18): https://www.you tube.com/watch?v=Uy8yLaoWybk.
- Learn more about diet culture from author and registered dietitian Christy Harrison in episode 22 on the *Impossible Beauty* podcast.
- Learn more about orthorexia and "When Healthy Isn't Helpful" from registered dietitian Victoria Myers in episode 77 on the *Impossible Beauty* podcast.
- Learn more about "Raising Kids in Diet Culture" from author and registered dietitian Sumner Brooks in episode 81 on the *Impossible Beauty* podcast.

- Learn more about "The Power of Advertising" from Jean Kilbourne in episode 23 on the *Impossible Beauty* podcast.
- Learn about "Beauty and Body Image" from Dr. Hillary McBride in episode 6 on the *Impossible Beauty* podcast.

4 SLOW SUICIDE

The hunger of the human heart that is unfed by what is authentic will go for what is inauthentic. If human beings need something vital badly enough, they may even destroy themselves trying to get it. —*Dallas Willard*

There's no doubt it was a low point. I wasn't myself. Something else had taken over. The thoughts that filled my mind, the desires that flooded my heart, were not at home within me. They were intruders, and yet in those moments, they held such power over me. For years and in more recent months, the inner chorus of *You're not good enough, Be thinner, Eat more perfect food,* and *No, that's too much food* steadily grew within me. That cold February evening in our bedroom, I sat alone. The demands that had steadily and then rapidly crescendoed in the recesses of my psyche had reached a new height.

Somehow being thinner had become an obsession—a devotion, even—of primary importance. It had nothing to do with vanity and everything to do with getting it right, with being successful at following society's rules for some warped kind of wellness—eating "perfect" food and being as thin and toned as possible, all while living an increasingly active lifestyle to that end. I had progressively shaped a life that pursued these things, and then the current shifted, and they pursued me. Somehow, they took over me, and that night I knew it.

As I stared at the familiar surroundings of our bedroom, my thoughts unraveled to a place I'm not happy or proud to admit. I was so obsessed with the rules, with pursuing thinness and fitness, that for some moments I thought it would be okay if I died as a result of being "successful" at this pursuit for perfection. I imagined that, in some way, that may even be an indicator of success—that my willpower and stamina to push past normal human needs and desires were a show of strength.

But a twisted show of strength.

See, you have to understand how utterly absurd that was. Growing up, I'd been handed everything a developing child and adolescent could ever want: a tremendously loving family, a supportive community, and friends. I was fortunate enough to receive a great education, and blessed to marry Jared, who is supportive and loving in all the ways I'd hoped a husband would be.

And I'd had this faith in God. Since I was little, I'd felt there was more to life, a certain mystery, and it enthralled me. The more I learned about God, the more I was drawn to knowing him more. As my faith in this mysterious God deepened, my sense of life having deep purpose and meaning grew too. So having spent thirty-one years being loved well and feeling that life held great purpose were pretty strong reasons for not destroying myself physically to pursue perfection, which in some warped way turned into pursuing emaciation.

I fully recognize how disturbed this sounds, and honestly, on that cold winter night, a part of me recognized it too. Thoughts like that startled me enough to awaken to my need for help. Those thoughts were not mine, not the thoughts of my true self. They weren't the ideas of the naturally curly-haired, adventure-seeking, music-loving, mostly introverted, passion-filled, lake-loving girl who wanted to live deeply and love well.

No, something had taken hold of me, and its intentions were for the destruction of my true self. Progressively, my multilayered, vibrant self had become like a one-dimensional robot on a mission of self-destruction. My obsession with self-deprivation and performance had narrowed my once expansive, purpose-filled vision for my life into cold, myopic tunnel vision.

Diminishing Returns

Only months later, after I'd settled into intensive treatment the following summer, did I realize this was the way of an eating disorder. This was its character and the trajectory of the disease. I realized it has a progressive nature to it, and the only certainty about that progression is that no particular number or standard will ever be good enough or perfect enough.

And so it takes and takes, and then it takes some more, until its demands and values have eclipsed your own authentic life purposes, goals, and desires. You see, the human mind and heart have only so much space, and this disorder is greedy for that sacred real estate. I've stood by and watched how it gladly and progressively takes over when given permission to do so, until it overshadows the unique beauties housed in the human mind and soul.

The disorder's ominous intentions became especially clear to me in the case of a woman I'll call Annalise. Annalise was simply beautiful, both inside and out. Her kindness and compassion toward others were so pure that it inspired you to deeper gentleness and warmth within yourself. She had short dark hair and big, innocent eyes.

Annalise and I met early on in my course of treatment, and I was thankful that we clicked immediately. As treatment progressed, I was glad to have her warm, empathic company in a number of groups along the way. Process groups and therapeutic meals felt more normal when

Annalise was alongside me; conversation flowed so easily. We could talk about how we were afraid of beef stroganoff but also about what we did over the past weekend.

The more I got to know her, the more I could sense a certain uneasiness just under the surface of what she presented to the world. Though I could clearly see the beauty in her, she was not at ease with herself. Oftentimes I noticed an instinct to reach out and "rescue" her in some way, to help her settle her internal unrest. But just as often, my own internal wisdom would rein my helper tendencies back in and remind me that it wasn't my job to save her and that saving was beyond the limits of my humanity.

All that to say that Annalise and I were friends, I was invested in her story, and I desired good things for her. I desired freedom for her.

One uneventful midweek day, I found myself once again in the earth-toned lobby of the clinic, listening to its quasi-soothing playlist and waiting for an appointment, when I noticed Annalise. She came over and greeted me like normal, but she was visibly upset. Her usual smile was nowhere to be seen; rather, a look of concern had taken over her commonly bright demeanor. I couldn't help but ask her what was wrong.

She responded with momentary silence, and her face now looked like she'd been punched in the gut. After another moment or two, she told me about the therapy session she'd just left. Her therapist told her if she didn't change what she was doing, she would die. The eating disorder would destroy her, literally.

You see, when your body is so starved of nutrition, some unfortunate and all-encompassing results take place physically, psychologically, cognitively, emotionally, relationally. Who you are, your healthy self, is progressively diminished in every dimension of your well-being as the disease progresses and nutrition wanes. Starvation or semi-starvation causes diminished concentration, decreased mental alertness, poor decision-making, depression, apathy, irritability, restlessness, and a loss of sense of humor. Food deprivation affects you socially as well, diminishing your desire to connect interpersonally. As may be expected, physical changes occur too—like a slowed heart rate, dizziness, blackouts, fatigue, and diminished physical strength.[1]

Not only can an eating disorder deplete a person's multilayered personality and physical vitality, but it does so in a progressive and accelerated fashion via their central control system, their brain. Certain shifts in the brain's neurotransmitter balance take place that not only sustain but also perpetuate elements of the disease, which "accelerate the disease process."[2] What potentially began as a pursuit of health, then, progressively turns into an outright coup—body, mind, and spirit.

Annalise's therapist was well aware of the disease's progressive and greedy ways. She'd likely observed other clients go down a similar path in their minds and hearts, slowly advancing the disorder's schemes from a distraction to a disease and at times to death. She knew its nefarious agenda, and it scared her.

It scared me too.

"True Self" Starvation

Though not all women struggling with body image are physically starving themselves, what if the system of American beauty is driving us all to a deeper starvation, one of the mind and the true self? Again, our society spends tremendous time, energy, and money sending implicit and explicit messages about our external, embodied selves. And as a society, we're not only obsessed with a person's aesthetic and physical presentation, but we value and rate them based on that presentation.

Again, I can't help but wonder about the repercussions of this reality on the internal lives of women, on our hearts and our souls. As we engage in various fixations—restricting calories, obsessing about what we eat, imagining physical imperfection—what might be occurring in our interior world?

My experience has revealed that the never satiated energies of these societal forces do indeed have similar trajectories and natures to those of an eating disorder—both are progressive, and both are life depleting. As we run the race to nowhere, pursuing society's goals for aesthetic perfection, we're also running from realizing our true self. This is a dismal reality, but it's not necessarily shocking, particularly when once again considering certain dynamics in American media and advertising.

> What if the system of American beauty is driving us all to a deeper starvation, one of the mind and the true self?

For instance, as authors Kate Mulvey and Melissa Richards discuss the evolving history of beauty in America, they name how the 1950s marked a time when females were becoming increasingly objectified in the media, as "it didn't matter if a girl's character might be questionable as long as she looked good."[3] Thus, mid-century America began to teach young girls and adult women that their innate sacred selfhood and pursuit of integrity weren't as important as looking good on the outside. So rather than spending time developing their character, they should invest their hearts and energy in their aesthetic appeal.

Jean Kilbourne additionally highlights how the increasingly thin standard for beauty in America progressively led women into taking extreme measures to meet that standard, engaging in things like plastic surgery and semi-starvation. In this way, America's value system for women, "reflected and reinforced by advertising," still today "urges girls to adopt a false self, to bury their real selves."[4] Women are engaging in behaviors that mute their internal cues as instinctual as hunger, and they would rather go under the knife than endure what's counter to societal perfection.

One theorist goes so far as to call the idealized images of "the good life" and "the perfect body" promoted in consumerist culture as a "cage within," as these ideals tend to drive people's behaviors, and yet their influence tends to escape their awareness. As a result, this cage's bars are "invisible and its power pernicious. . . . While people believe they are expressing their selves and attaining happiness, they are, in fact, developing, monitoring, and molding their identities with respect to unrealistic ideals promoted by consumer culture through advertising."[5]

We've become so entrapped by American standards for beauty and the lifestyle associated with that standard that unhelpful and even harmful behaviors and beliefs regarding food, exercise, and body image are normalized. They're so idealized that many may believe these skin-deep endeavors are the epitome of their existence.

Instead of women paying attention to their preferences and nuanced intuitions, they allow society to inform them of what they really *should* like, things like low-carb health food and Pilates. Both the eating disorder and our society's script for perfection, then, have an agenda for how things *should* go and what women *should* do. In this way, "mass communication has made possible a kind of national peer pressure that erodes private and individual values and standards."[6] So often, the latest program and product are the cultural *shoulds* of the day, the adult peer pressure that is cultural beauty.

Often, as we strive to achieve the ideal body type, our inner critic must grow louder in order to enforce certain "rules" regarding food and exercise. And as that voice grows, our inner voice of wisdom, compassion, and intuition is drowned out. Our individual instincts and values are eclipsed by an outside agenda, one that is alien to our own internal voice. So while Pilates may not be nefarious in and of itself, it is unhelpful when Pilates or any other kind of exercise is packaged as the gateway to toned aesthetic perfection and implicitly sold as the yellow brick road to universal acceptance and internal euphoria.

Don't get me wrong. I'm all for eating mindfully and nourishing our bodies with nutrient-rich foods. I'm also a great advocate for moving our bodies regularly, as I believe we've been created to celebrate and engage life in our physicality. But when behaviors, beliefs, or thought processes around these things become fixations and obsessions and no longer serve us and our overall well-being, they're problematic. We somehow come to serve them rather than their serving us. Our minds can become fraught and distressed with self-judgments about what we ate or didn't eat or *should* eat, how much we exercised or didn't exercise, or what our body should or shouldn't look like.

This is not life-giving. This is not freedom. And for many American women, the fixations, assessments, and judgments are so loud that they become principal guides in their lives, led by society's agenda and values versus the guidance of their own internal world.

The drowning out of the sacred inner voice, a person's true self, is tragic to me. What is most unique and beautiful can become progressively diminished, unnoticed, forgotten. And what happens en masse when women progressively and increasingly become entranced and led by society's warped, guiding light of "beauty," when we sacrifice attunement with our unique selfhood for societal demands for seeking perfection? Without diversity in our likes and dislikes, passions, pursuits, personalities, strengths, and unique challenges, what are we but bland, passionless lemmings in a world colorless and void of vitality?

That sort of bland reality, void of the richness of individual diversity, is so tragic to me, because I believe we've been created to be so much more.

You see, I believe in a loving God, as in so loving that his nature is love and his being radiates goodness. I also believe that good and loving God envisioned and created us in our own unique beauty and varied quirkiness. Like an artist, a poet, or sculptor thoughtfully and with great care creates something new and sacred, so I believe

God created each one of us. I believe we are each uniquely crafted and so uniquely loved and intimately appreciated by our creator for the distinct contours of our inmost being.

Author Parker Palmer expands on this idea of the "true self" or the distinct shape of the "sacred soul" we each possess: "Biblical faith calls it the image of God in which we are all created. Thomas Merton calls it true self. Quakers call it the inner light, or 'that of God' in every person. The humanist tradition calls it identity and integrity. No matter what you call it, it is a pearl of great price."[7]

Palmer goes on to note the diminishing effect a society can have on the true self, this "pearl of great price":

> As young people, we are surrounded by expectations that may have little to do with who we really are, expectations held by people who are not trying to discern our selfhood but to fit us into slots . . . we are trained away from true self toward images of acceptability; under social pressures like racism and sexism our original shape is deformed beyond recognition; and we ourselves, driven by fear, too often betray true self to gain the approval of others. We are disabused of original giftedness in the first half of our lives. Then—if we are awake, aware, and able to admit our loss—we spend the second half trying to recover and reclaim the gift we once possessed.[8]

We encounter many forces that can diminish us. I've seen up close how a culture that teaches us that our worth is in our thinness or our aesthetic flawlessness damages the depths of our inner world. This message diminishes the true self and serves as a colossal distraction from nurturing and noticing what is eternal within us. In this way, all the frenzied marketing and rhetoric about a woman's physical self is assuredly not confined to external realities.

Rather, the problem of epidemic negative body image and eating disorders in America is not strictly a physical problem; it's a problem that penetrates every layer of our being. It's a problem that is psychological, emotional, and assuredly spiritual. In my own story, at distinctive points I had glimpses into the holistic takeover occurring, and that February evening was certainly one of them. I knew I had to find a new way forward, a new way of defining my identity, my worth, because this way wasn't working—and because it was killing me physically, psychologically, spiritually.

Even in my very early recovery, I realized the disorder's intentions were for my destruction. I also realized that, in some twisted way, *I* was involved in my self-destruction. I hadn't realized that an eating disorder is like a slow suicide, rendering the life-joy and vitality of its sufferers lifeless. I observed and obeyed as the internal dialogue of the eating disorder turned from one of a "friend" coaching me on attaining cultural ideals for food and exercise, into an internal dictator demanding less food and more exercise.

> An eating disorder is like a slow suicide, rendering the life-joy and vitality of its sufferers lifeless.

Under the gravitational pull of the dictator's exhortations, I failed to realize what I was losing as I tirelessly tried to meet its growing demands. And when you aren't eating enough or you live in an unbalanced fashion, your brain and body start to do some strange things.

For one, nutrition is tied to serotonin. So for instance, when you aren't eating enough carbohydrates or fat, it's easier to get entrenched in the "dictator's" demands around food, as low levels of serotonin are associated with obsessive thought processes. Furthermore, the disorder has a way of usurping your identity, hobbies, and values. As you surrender these former ways of passing time to the demands of the disorder, your former self is gradually eclipsed.

Then the ante continues to be upped, and simply put, the demands of the disorder become your life, and your ability to meet those ever-increasing, never-satisfied demands become the foundation for your sense of worth and identity.

At some point in my treatment, this epiphany hit me: The eating disorder's increasing demands were leading to the loss of my identity, energy, vitality, values, life balance . . . the list goes on. It was taking away the life I'd once known. And literally speaking, if I continued to try to meet its demands, it wouldn't stop until it had taken my physical life as well.

I knew I had to make efforts to walk upstream against the current that had been over a decade in the making.

I FOR REFLECTION

1. Have you noticed any unhelpful yet normalized cultural beliefs regarding food, exercise, and body image? If so, what are they?

2. How might these unhelpful beliefs impact a person's overall well-being (physical, cognitive, emotional, relational, spiritual)? How might they be impacting yours?

❙ FOR FURTHER STUDY

- Learn more about reconnecting with our bodies and our intuition from registered dietitian and coauthor of the bestselling book *Intuitive Eating: A Revolutionary Anti-Diet Approach*, Evelyn Tribole, in episode 29 on the *Impossible Beauty* podcast.

5 THE VILLAIN

The devil's finest trick is to persuade you that he does not exist.
—*Charles Baudelaire*

Any story worth telling has a villain, a mastermind, set on destroying the story's hero or heroine. The villain tends to be clever and full of all sorts of schemes. And the story of American beauty is no exception. In this story, I have seen and felt how evil itself is its crafty villain. An adversary set against true beauty, goodness, and our thriving.

And as both a spectator and participant in this story, I've also seen with certain clarity that the villain has a powerful minion called shame—that perceived sense that we just aren't good enough, that something is wrong with us, that *we* are wrong. Shame is so toxic and troublesome because it goes to the core of who we are. It's not just about that thing we did or failed to do but what it has to do with our worth as a human.

Essentially, shame puts my worth and my internal "okay-ness" in question. I cannot be at peace with myself if I believe I'm not "right."

Several years ago, a therapist mentor of mine told me that shame is a spiritual force. She noted that when she's talking with a client, the atmosphere shifts as her client's perceived unworthiness enters the room. Her sentiments on shame have stuck with me. I now watch for that shift with clients, with friends, and in my own thought life and behavior. When shame is on the scene and someone's sense of being "good enough" comes into question, a certain unravelling begins.

If shame is the spiritual, unquiet energy fueling the engine of American beauty culture, fighting against it feels decidedly intimidating. If one client's shame makes a decisive shift in a therapy room, millions of American women believing, thinking, and behaving as though they aren't good enough is like a tidal wave of shame.

And tragically, some may conclude they will *never* be good enough.

Psychiatrist and author Dr. Curt Thompson goes one step further, not only stating that shame is spiritual but that it has a distinct agenda. He goes on to cite the biblical narrative for his belief that both forces of good and evil are at work in the world. God is at work to create and re-create, to renew, authoring all that is good, beautiful, and loving. Conversely, forces of evil are at work, and, as Thompson says it, "evil has wielded shame as a primary weapon to see to it" that God's original intentions for "emerging goodness, beauty and joy" in the world never come to fruition.[1]

> Millions of American women believing, thinking, and behaving as though they aren't good enough is like a tidal wave of shame.

Shame, then, is a tool evil employs to taint and disfigure our relationship with God, ourselves, and one another. Furthermore, shame gets in the way of our realizing and enacting our true identity and calling: to use our gifts and creativity to reflect and maximize God's love, beauty, and goodness in our lives, our communities, and the world. It could even be posed that evil is at work to disfigure the concept of beauty itself, misdirecting our hearts and energies toward something fleeting versus the eternal.

Thompson goes on to say that shame "is both a source and a result of evil's active assault on God's creation, and a way for evil to try to

hold out until the new heaven and earth appear at the consumma-
tion of history."[2]

In this worldview, ever since Adam and Eve ate from the Tree
of Knowledge of Good and Evil (as told in the book of Genesis at
the start of the biblical narrative and resulting in a chain reaction of
brokenness entering the world), evil has been working to diminish
God's good work and purposes while, at the same time, God has been
tirelessly working to reclaim his creation.

A Glimmer of Hope

That's a lot. A lot of theology and a lot of heaviness. Let's pause a
moment for the hope of a promise.

The biblical narrative also includes a momentous glimmer of
hope—the promise that one day God will reclaim the world in a significant and final way, that there will be no more evil or suffering,
and that the love, joy, and connection God purposed for humanity
will be realized.

God's shalom, which existed before the fall (the whole Adam and
Eve event in Genesis 3), will once again be realized at that time. The
concept of shalom is synonymous with our right relatedness with
God, others, the systems we're a part of, and God's good creation.
It also includes well-being within the human soul. Put another way,
"Shalom means universal flourishing, wholeness, and delight. It is
the way things ought to be."[3] There's flourishing on every level of
creation. In this reality, justice reigns as well. And so this flourishing
is for all people.

Though most English-language Bibles translate *shalom* to *peace*,
shalom goes far beyond the notion of an absence of conflict. The
idea of flourishing as shalom is a significant theme in the Old Testament, encompassing themes of reconciliation, contentment, and right

relationship between nations and peoples. Long story short, shalom "is the way God intended things to be when he created the universe."[4]

Until then, it's humanity's job, the work of the true self, to realize our true identity as God's beloved children and take our place in his rescue mission for humanity. It's our mission to enact shalom in our spheres of influence. In this way, our lives are part of a much larger, epic story of redemption. And finding our place in that narrative helps us realize that we're connected to God, to others, and to creation in significant and inextricable ways.

In the midst of that narrative, Dr. Thompson would say that shame, as a minion of evil, has been and will continue to try to thwart that plan of renewal and redemption at every corner.

Spiritual Realities

Without sounding too archaic or fantastical, what if spiritual realities and dynamics are indeed at play in the world? Could it be that love, hope, joy, and even shame transcend mere emotion, crossing into the realm of spirit and soul? Author and Franciscan friar Richard Rohr states that "our problem now is that we seriously doubt that there is any vital reality to the spiritual world . . . the universe is not inherently enchanted, as it was for the ancients."[5] In this way, he says, "our mass cultural trance is like scales over our eyes. We see only with the material eye."[6]

This side of the Enlightenment movement of the seventeenth and eighteenth centuries, which heralded reason as the primary source of knowledge, we Westerners too often believe that since things of a spiritual nature can't be scientifically analyzed and proven, they're not valid, not real. We think we know better than ancient societies and people from other parts of the world. But do we? Is this disbelief, this discounting of all things spiritual, truly serving us well?

72

There is so much more to life than meets the eye. In fact, the Bible attests to this good versus evil, light versus dark reality.

New Testament writer the apostle Paul stated that "our struggle is not against flesh and blood, but against the rulers, against the authorities, against the powers of this dark world and against the spiritual forces of evil in the heavenly realms."[7]

The apostle Peter warned, "Be alert and of sober mind. Your enemy the devil prowls around like a roaring lion looking for someone to devour."[8]

And Jesus himself lived with this worldview throughout his ministry, seeking to come against darkness in its every form. Bringing wholeness and healing to hurting people and broken systems. Inaugurating a new chapter of bringing God's redemptive action to a broken world. As Jesus stated, "The thief comes only to steal and kill and destroy; I have come that they may have life and have it to the full."[9]

Amid the rubble of our current broken (and post-Enlightenment) reality, such spiritual realities may be challenging to access at times, but I believe in a God who lovingly and meticulously created our very body, soul, and being. And the Spirit or the essence of that God is all around us. We only need eyes to see it. Look a little closer at the red-gold sunset, the awe-inspiring breakers of the ocean, the complexity of an infant, the attentive love between parents and their child. Something sacred is in our midst, a beauty that cannot be denied or diluted.

And like Dr. Thompson, I also believe there is a true villain, a real counterforce of darkness in the world seeking to interrupt the chorus of the world's beauty with the refrain of suffering, disease, and heartbreak. I believe it because I've seen it, felt it. It resonates so deeply with my lived experience—the only explanation for the mismatched collision of heartbreak and elation, devastation and wonder, hatred and love.

Interestingly enough, it seems that human hearts crave an expression of this good versus evil reality at an intuitive level. Our creative nature bears witness to this instinctive awareness in expressions of light and darkness in art and music, or in the more glaring, overt battles in the *Star Wars*, *Lord of the Rings*, and *Chronicles of Narnia* series or the vast array of superhero movies. We may not have casual chats with our coworkers or friends about these constructs, but we seem to have an awareness of them on at least a subconscious level.

So what does it mean for our seemingly mundane lives if indeed something epic is going on beneath the surface and very much in our midst, a story of light versus darkness in which the dark forces of shame seek to destroy our true selves? If we were to come awake to this sort of storyline, I imagine life would seem much more monumental than we ever imagined. We may also seek to become increasingly aware of the villainous forces that seek to fracture our soul's well-being, our unity with others, and our connection with our creator.

Collateral Damage

Now back to evil's minion, shame. If shame is a tool used to disintegrate and diminish, I'd say that when it comes to the system of how we value women in America, it's doing a pretty bang-up job. Women comparing themselves to the thin ideal and tirelessly seeking aesthetic perfection to gain worth in our society reeks of shame and its effects on so many levels.

When women are convinced that their body, the physical embodiment of their being, doesn't measure up, all sorts of fallout can occur to their self-esteem, self-assessment, and mental health. What's particularly tragic is when they in a sense "cut off" from their body. Due to body shame, they no longer pay attention to the cues and intuitions their body is communicating. Their embodied experience is no longer holistic but fragmented. The life they were meant to enjoy body, mind, and soul is diminished because they're largely divorced from their embodied experience.

How can we enjoy the gifts of embodiment—sight, sound, touch—when we're rejecting our physicality as a whole?

This is even more complicated when considering how the social comparison game fractures relationships. When we fall into the trap of measuring ourselves against others to gain a perceived sense of worth, our relationships are ruptured as judgment and a sort of social ranking taint the beauty of relational unity.

> How can we enjoy the gifts of embodiment—sight, sound, touch—when we're rejecting our physicality as a whole?

Even more, on a larger societal level, valuing women for how their bodies align with a thin ideal has all kinds of villainous effects. No longer are we valued as unique, holistically embodied sacred beings but only for our aesthetic appeal. A woman is *only* her body, and we're taught via advertising and the media that it's to be assessed, judged, and lusted after. As far as our society is concerned, a woman is only as good as her physical shell.

I believe whole systems are influenced by the undercurrents of evil in the world. And when it comes to the systems upholding the values of American beauty, not only do they marginalize us as a whole, but they work hand in hand to personally deliver the message that our embodied self just isn't good enough.

It seems that message has been received.

The Sneakiness

Early on in life, we learn that any villain worth their salt is both sneaky and sinister. The villain will implement all kinds of craftiness to take down the story's hero. And if evil's task is indeed to take down God's beloved, I have seen some of the craftiest, twisted tactics in the progressive takeover of an eating disorder in a person's life.

Several narrative therapists—practitioners who use a therapeutic approach that helps a person externalize their problem—compiled women's journal entries regarding their eating disorder experience, and a similar trajectory emerged. Numerous clients wrote about how the disorder began as a friend to help them accomplish their goal of losing weight, but then progressively turned into their captor in a dream-turned-nightmare. The disorder shifted shapes as they were invited into its gravitational pull with progressive ease, and then it became a tyrant as the disease progressed.

Once the disorder has its talons firmly secured in the life of its prisoner, it tries to establish an outright takeover. That total coup of body, mind, and spirit I mentioned earlier.

One woman wrote:

> *Anorexia tells you your name is Anorexia and you forget who you are.*
> 1. *You are not a person, you are an object, a thing, a body to be deprived of pleasure to be tortured and starved.*
> 2. *I will steal your name and replace it with Anorexia.*
> 3. *I will steal your soul and replace it with Anorexia.*
> 4. *I will steal your voice.*[10]

Loved ones of those struggling with an eating disorder describe the disorder's progressive, all-encompassing takeover like this: "It's as if a force without form or substance has taken possession of the person." And the aforementioned narrative therapists say this about their clients: "As anorexia/bulimia proceeds, these women become less and less substantial as people until finally the person they were becomes almost invisible."[11]

There's a progressive nature to usurping the true self. The eating disorder knows this well, and the villain knows this well. That nature is sneaky, and it's sinister. That is its craft.

My personal experience in intensive treatment has taught me some additional truths about the craftiness of an eating disorder. So often I would look around a group room and think what amazing women I was with. And I noticed some sweeping commonalities among them. Kind. Sensitive. Internalizing. Caretaking. Thoughtful. Nurturing. Intelligent. Treatment often felt like the failed Perfectionist Club. These women were so conscientious and had such desire to do life "right." To do food and exercise "right" and check all the other boxes for being a kind, moral, good person. They wanted to love others so well, but somewhere they'd lost track of what loving themselves looked and felt like.

> There's a progressive nature to usurping the true self. The eating disorder knows this well, and the villain knows this well.

What I found so sneaky about the eating disorder is that, in such a distorted way, trying to do it right had turned against these women and against me.

This disorder, often based in perfectionism and anxiety, is a way to destroy women (and men) in a backward way. It turns doing it right into an obsession with food, exercise, and all the rest. Oftentimes as these women tried to be there for everyone else in their life, they lost touch with their own needs. And eerily enough, the disorder is a fine way to numb out your own needs, reinforcing the deceit that you can do it all.

Not in a million years would I have thought that being a sensitive, nurturing person could be overdone and turned against these women and me. But as it turns out, it seems the villain can use the desire to do it right as fertile soil for our own progressive destruction.

Again, there's the sneakiness.

If it is indeed evil's job to deplete life and destroy all that is good, beautiful, and lovely, it's certainly making headway when it comes to eating disorders. And I would argue it's doing its job in the "never enough" messaging laced in American beauty culture as well. In either case, the gravity, subtlety, and sneakiness of its advance in a person's life has been startling to me.

The sneakiness of the villain reminds me of mammon. Jesus talks about mammon in the form of money in his Sermon on the Mount in Matthew 6:24. He says, "No one can serve two masters. Either you will hate the one and love the other, or you will be devoted to the one and despise the other. You cannot serve both God and money."

"Mammon" is often used to describe the "debasing influence of material wealth."[12] Somehow, gaining wealth has a gravity to it; it has a way of seizing our devotion. Mammon is also known to be personified, with medieval writers commonly interpreting it as an evil demon or god.[13]

Pastor and author Greg Boyd broadens this meaning to include wealth or anything else that holds our devotion, and pursuing mammon often looks like "winning at the world's game." An additional indicator of mammon is that it feeds on discontentment, and that discontentment is fueled with a lie ("You will be happy when" or "You will find acceptance if"). The problem is mammon doesn't deliver. It leaves us "perpetually hungry, striving after more."[14]

Boyd's reflections on mammon could not be more spot-on when it comes to American beauty and diet culture. It stirs up shame, instigates a race to nowhere, and leaves us empty. And there's also a spiritual nature to it. It's subtle, sneaky, and has gravity. As Boyd says, "The more of it you have [or achieve] the more of you it has."[15]

Whether it's the "never enough" gravity of American beauty and diet culture, or of an eating disorder, there's an additional layer to these undercurrents of evil in the world. Something more is happening, and it's an urgent matter. When women are very much distracted, pursuing the demands of an eating disorder or chasing the "never enough" demands of American beauty, they're starving their true self.

And if Dr. Thompson is right and we're playing a game much bigger than ourselves, awaking to our true self is essential. Because our role is pivotal. We have good, beautiful, creative, and lovely things to do, and we can't do them if we're starving ourselves, literally and spiritually.

> We have good, beautiful, creative, and lovely things to do, and we can't do them if we're starving ourselves, literally and spiritually.

God is tirelessly working to redeem every square inch of creation, to bring about the fullness of beauty, goodness, and shalom. And we have been invited along in that mission. We have one life to live, and there is sacred work for us to do. So when we fight against the forces of evil, an eating disorder, shame, or the lie that we or our bodies will never be enough, we're also fighting for goodness, and we're fighting for Light.

The Warden

I called her "the warden." Not to her face, of course, but my dad and I used to watch those movies from the fifties and sixties that took place in some gloomy POW camp or prison, and they often featured a rugged warden or guard who had particular clout. They had authority because they were simultaneously feared and respected.

Well, that was the case with Eva. That's not her real name, but I always thought her actual name was just as understated for such a powerful person.

While we ate, it was the role of the therapists to process struggles that arose or call out any disordered eating behaviors they saw. Some therapists would make a quiet side comment or wait to check in with you after a meal. Not Eva. Women avoided sitting near her because she would boldly name what she saw in real time, mid-meal and usually quite publicly.

I actually really liked her; she had great insights and seemed to care about her clients. But she was blunt, and because self-deceit and denial are popular accomplices to an eating disorder, calling their bluff was a bit jarring. But Eva wasn't about to let comments like "Oh, I just don't like pizza" or "Pasta makes my stomach hurt" slide. Nope, she was like a heat-seeking missile for BS, and that's pretty scary when you don't want anyone to see the depths of the disorder's hold on you. Not even yourself.

But the more I watched Eva and listened to her comments and questions, the more I stopped fearing her. I was even drawn to her. I also noticed that other women were drawn to Eva the longer they were in treatment and making strides in fighting against the disorder. Slowly, my respect and appreciation for her grew not so much for what she was for (calling us out) but for what she was against (that which did not bring us life). She was a master at noticing, calling forth, and naming the latter.

You see, like some of our other therapists, Eva had been where we were. She'd fought against the eating disorder years before, so she knew the life-depleting, personality-depleting, sneaky ways of the disorder. As an insider, she knew how to ask us questions, to challenge us to see the web of deceit we'd been caught up in.

Even more, she knew there was so much more to life for each one of us. We were intricate souls with multifaceted beauty and God-given gifts. Somehow, we'd been overtaken by the currents of perfectionism and obsession, and she knew the road we had to take to reclaim our true selves. She understood the fight against the "never enough" message and the lies of American beauty. In many ways, she was fighting for my true self before I knew I needed to. Progressively and eventually, I realized what Eva already knew.

And I started fighting back.

| FOR REFLECTION

1. What in this chapter is striking to you? Did it challenge you in any way or cause any shifts in your thinking? How so?

2. Brené Brown defines shame as the "intensely painful feeling or experience of believing that we are flawed and therefore unworthy of love and belonging."[16] What is it like to consider shame as a minion of evil? Can you think of any specific ways shame fractures our soul's well-being, our unity with others, and our connection with our creator? If so, please name them.

▌ FOR FURTHER STUDY

- Learn more about "Connecting with Our Bodies, Connecting with Each Other" from spiritual director and the founder and executive director of Anam Cara Ministries, Tara Owens, on episode 86 of the *Impossible Beauty* podcast.

6 THE MORALITY OF JUDGMENT

Our only job is to love, not judge. —*Greg Boyd*

It was the beginning of an odd and unfortunate rite of passage. There we were in our high school's women's bathroom—me, the new kid, and some fellow sophomore acquaintances I hoped would soon be friends—when I was first invited into a new way of seeing my body.

The other girls were lined up in front of the mirror, assessing their physical selves—what was too big, what was too small, and how they planned to adjust their lunches that day to help address whatever they considered visually unpleasant or imperfect.

I remember standing back, bewildered. I was a bit of a late bloomer, shall we say, and at times crossing into semi-tomboy territory. So this whole drawn-out charade in front of the mirror was a bit confusing to me.

At that point in my life, I used the mirror only to make sure my hair wasn't too frizzy or out of place and that my outfit was generally neat looking. I wasn't so sure about this ritual of drawn-out analyzing and physical self-scrutiny. It really felt like a waste of time. I mean, I would have much preferred they'd be getting to know the new kid than taking an exaggerated amount of time for this pre-lunch aesthetic self-check.

I felt a bit awkward and gangly growing up, but as a young teen, I hardly ever thought about my physical presence in the world. My body helped me run, play soccer, water-ski, ride my bike, and walk to school, but rarely did I consider whether my physical self was displeasing to others.

The more I encountered and soon adopted the art of self-judgment, however, the more that carefree experience of my embodied self waned. Oh, I knew the art of self-judgment in other realms of my life, but until now it had failed to infiltrate how I viewed my physical self in any significant way. Yet experiencing similar mirror rituals throughout high school and college—and all sorts of side comments about others' perceived physical imperfections or shortcomings—the relationship I had with my body progressively and slowly shifted.

I wonder if you had a similar experience.

Soon, I no longer viewed my body as the vessel I used to do all the activities I loved but as an object that needed to conform to the cultural aesthetic "perfection" I'd adopted as the gold standard. And when I noticed something I thought didn't conform, I learned it made all the sense in the world to be annoyed and frustrated and make whatever changes necessary to alter that imperfection. The relationship I established with my body steadily became wrought with self-scrutiny and increasing efforts of self-control. I became a perfectionistic dictator toward my sacred embodied self.

> As a young teen, rarely did I consider whether my physical self was displeasing to others.

These rituals of self-assessment and self-judgment have become a way of life, a way of being, for all too many women in America. Indeed, it's as if it has become a rite of passage for us females to learn to judge and scrutinize our physical self. At an increasingly young age, we learn that our bodies are objects to be analyzed, judged, and tweaked. And along the way, we're introduced to devices like Fitbits and weight scales to assist us in our physical self-assessment and its corresponding goals—though their numbers often give us more fuel for self-judgment.

The tendency for us to scrutinize our bodies has become so prevalent that social scientists even have a term for it: Fat Talk. Fat Talk is the tendency for women to bond with other women by speaking negatively about the size or shape of their bodies,[1] which often occurs when they're trying to comfort someone else by putting themselves down or to create commonality.[2]

We're also socialized to believe that certain foods are permissible and even praiseworthy, while others are considered bad—as if foods have a certain moral value to them. We then learn to take on or absorb the morality of the foods we eat, learning to make comments about how guilty we feel for eating *x*, *y*, or *z*. We somehow become "bad" for eating whatever we did, and suddenly shame infiltrates our everyday experiences with food.

> It's as if it has become a rite of passage for us females to learn to judge and scrutinize our physical self.

These sorts of judgment-based relationships with our bodies and with food are decidedly destructive. I wonder if they've been destructive in your story as well; clearly, they have been in mine. Learning to make harsh judgments about my body and about the nourishment I gave it were cornerstone to the construction of the eating disorder's stronghold in my life.

The Tragedy

If judgment can be so destructive, why do we do it? Why does judging ourselves and judging others seem to run rampant in the human mind and our casual conversations? Dr. Curt Thompson also gives us some insight here, regarding our addiction to judgment, or as he defines it, "the spirit of condemnation or condescension with which we analyze or critique something, whether ourselves or someone or something else."[3] Not surprisingly, Thompson brings us back to shame. Simply put, "Shamed people shame people."[4]

Essentially, our judgment of others is rooted in our own self-judgment. Because we have so much trouble being or feeling or looking "good enough," we get caught up in all sorts of criticism, critique, and judgment toward ourselves. And then we do our neighbors and friends the favor (please note sarcasm) of using that same critical eye to judge and assess their looks, their behavior, their beliefs, and so on. So according to Thompson, your mom was largely right: we tend to judge others based on our own insecurities, or stated even more accurately, based on our own shame.

Because shame abounds, so does judgment. We judge ourselves, we judge others, and we judge them for judging us. Critiquing and assessing others sweeps through human relationships like wildfire. The tragedy here is that in the flurry of these shame-based wildfires, we set up systems of worth for people based on cultural assessments for what is considered good or preferable. As in we literally value certain people more than others for how they measure up in our cultural value system.

Let's look more closely at two sad factors in this tragedy—(1) social hierarchy and its constructs, and (2) the Body Mass Index (BMI) and the diet industry.

Social hierarchy and its constructs—then and now

The reality of social hierarchy is an ugly one—one sacred being is considered and often treated as more valuable or more respectable according to what the larger culture deems valuable. This is and has been true for gender, race, ethnicity, socioeconomic status, and body shape and size as well. Certain conclusions or assumptions are made about a person based on the size or shape of their body. And in general, again, women are respected and valued based on how thin they are. Such a judgmental system is tragic, and it's immoral.

This social hierarchy based on body shape and size has historical roots no less ugly than our current reality. In her book *Anti-Diet*, Christy Harrison expounds on the roots of diet culture and the history of how some bodies have come to be valued over others. For one, Harrison explains how as more immigrants flooded into America during the mid to late 1800s, the white middle class sought out ways to maintain a dominant position in society. At that time, the rise of a thinner ideal emerged in part to distinguish the middle class from the "stout, sturdy" immigrant. Thinness became an indicator of social status.[5]

Additionally, amid developing theories on race and evolution, a racial hierarchy emerged during the nineteenth century. Some groups were categorized as more civilized or evolved than others. Not surprisingly, the men doing the categorizing, largely white men of northern European descent, placed themselves at the top of the hierarchy. So while evolutionary theory had its helpfulness, it also served to uphold the status quo when it came to exerting domination over certain people groups.[6]

Harrison further explains how these nineteenth-century scientists started cataloging various societies' cultural norms and physical traits. Author and sociologist Sabrina Strings gives us further insight into that categorization system in her book *Fearing the Black Body*. She describes how fatness became linked with blackness, as the feature of a larger body was said to occur more frequently among the people of color these scientists observed. Fatness was seen as an indicator of savagery and racial inferiority. As Strings states it, "The racialized female body became legible, a form of 'text' from which racial superiority and inferiority were read."[7]

Meanwhile, supposedly thinness appeared more often in white people, men, and aristocrats. As a result of this sham hierarchy, larger bodies were seen as inferior to the point that white, middle-class Protestant women were warned against excessive eating, as it would lead to having a body more like African or Irish women.[8]

The human addiction to judgment continues into contemporary times. For instance, this value system based on body size or shape includes a trend known as weight bias and has been demonstrated in numerous studies spanning from children to adults alike. One study demonstrated that teachers assume overweight students to be less likely to succeed at work, untidy, overly emotional, and more likely to have family problems compared to "normal" weighted students.[9] According to several decades of research, this sort of weight bias crosses over into adulthood and into various domains of life, including health care, employment, the media, interpersonal relationships, and schools.[10]

Such research demonstrates trends like doctors spending less time examining overweight patients and engaging in less discussion with them,[11] overweight job applicants being less likely to be hired (especially female applicants),[12] and overweight employees earning less than their equally qualified, more "normal" weighted peers (this salary difference being greater for overweight women than for overweight men).[13]

There's even a theory called the *What is beautiful is good effect*, suggesting that people considered attractive are assumed to have positive character traits. One study found that attractiveness in Disney movies was positively correlated with friendliness, moral virtue, romantic involvement, and socioeconomic status.[14] So a person's worth and character are often assumed by the image they portray. And generally, thinness is associated with "self-discipline, self-control, and niceness."[15]

Thinness, then, has become a mark of morality. And this assumption may derive from its association with historic Christian examples of saintly virtue and self-denial.[16]

Conversely, being overweight has become associated with laziness. This correlation gained particular momentum in the United States during the early twentieth century, when work became less labor intensive and more sedentary. During this time, materialism and leisure activities also grew more prevalent. Amid these changing cultural dynamics, dieting became a way to showcase a person's supposed moral character[17]—a way to demonstrate their self-discipline, perseverance, and other such culturally exalted traits.

If you're anything like me, these trends and findings may have you fuming. Not only are they morally wrong, but they're based on faulty assumptions. For one, such judgments ignore the fact that bodies are naturally diverse and diversity is beautiful. Such judgments also fail to recognize that bodies can be healthy in many shapes and sizes.

Think of the varied types of bodies you see in sports like football, rugby, soccer, and wrestling. There are so many examples of athletic and/or healthy people who don't necessarily meet slim and "flawless" cultural ideals. Women like renowned novelist and long-distance cyclist Jennifer Weiner and long-distance ultra-runner Mirna Valerio say that their bodies do not fit athletic stereotypes, and yet both are experienced endurance athletes. I've also heard stories from women whose heart rate slowed or they had difficulty conceiving because of their disordered relationship with food while considered normal weighted according to societal standards. Simply put, healthy does not have a single look.

The Body Mass Index (BMI) and the diet industry

One additional consideration on the topic of health, body shape, and size is the current Body Mass Index (BMI) measure for categorizing people as normal weight, overweight, or underweight, with normal considered ideal.

This measurement is problematic in and of itself. As Christy Harrison explains, it was developed in the 1830s by a Belgian astronomer (yes, an *astronomer*) named Adolphe Quetelet "as a way to test whether the laws of probability could be applied to human beings at the population level. It was created as a statistical exercise, not a medical instrument, and was never intended for clinical use."[18] Additionally, Quetelet developed his equation exclusively using a white, European population, thus lacking differences in average body size in other ethnic groups.[19]

Despite the problematic basis for the BMI measure, Harrison goes on to reference data from a modern-day meta-analysis that showed that those in the "overweight" category actually had the lowest mortality risk of any group on the BMI chart.[20,21] Thus, even using this outdated instrument, there's data refuting the faulty conclusion that health equals a certain size or weight.

This whole issue of BMI becomes increasingly frustrating when considering the so-called obesity epidemic. As Harrison explains it, in 1998 millions of Americans were suddenly "overweight" or "obese" overnight when "the National Institutes of Health (NIH), the U.S. federal agency in charge of setting the official BMI categories for American guidelines, released a report changing its thresholds for what is considered 'overweight' and 'obese.' People suddenly moved into new, higher BMI categories without having gained any weight whatsoever, simply because the cutoffs had changed."[22]

The reason this is so frustrating comes to light when considering the political origins of this change. The shift in guidelines was based on a report the World Health Organization (WHO) had published two years earlier, primarily written by another organization called the International Obesity Task Force (IOTF). The IOTF was funded largely by F. Hoffman-La Roche and Abbott Laboratories, two pharmaceutical companies that manufacture weight-loss drugs. As Harrison describes it,

> The IOTF's purpose was to lobby for and create science that supports the interests of the pharmaceutical industry—and, of course, lowering BMI cutoffs so that millions more Americans think they have a "weight problem" is definitely in the interest of pharmaceutical companies selling weight-loss drugs.[23]

Furthermore, in his 2005 book *Fat Politics*, political scientist J. Eric Oliver expounds on this cozy relationship between so-called obesity experts and their deep ties to the diet industry: "It is difficult to find any major figure in the field of obesity research . . . who does not have some type of financial tie to a pharmaceutical or weight-loss company."[24]

Thus, the common implicit and explicit message from diet culture that thinness equals health isn't as cut and dried or true as has been communicated to us. Additionally, this narrowly defined external and aesthetic basis for health misses the fact that we are holistic beings made up of our cognition, our emotions, our spirit, and our connection to others. I've seen many instances where shame or obsession—casualties of diet culture—have severely damaged or stood in the way of a person's cognitive, emotional, relational, or spiritual well-being. This one-dimensional approach to health is harmful, inaccurate, and often fueled by ulterior, economically based motives.

A More Supportive View of Size and Health

At this point you might be wondering how on earth we can pursue health without the influence of diet culture. When my eyes were first opened to these realities, I found myself wondering the same thing. Thankfully, there is an approach to health care that is weight-inclusive and anti-diet, designed to help people take care of their bodies without trying to shrink them. This approach that honors natural body diversity is called Health At Every Size (HAES), and it includes the following principles:

- Providing weight-inclusive care that accepts and respects body diversity and refuses to demonize certain weights or elevate others;
- Supporting health-related policies and practices that help people's well-being in a truly holistic sense, including their physical, emotional, social, spiritual, and economic needs;
- Refusing to blame people for their health outcomes;
- Acknowledging the biases that health-care providers hold, and working to end discrimination and stigma based on body size or any other form of identity;
- Providing respectful care that acknowledges the intersecting identities people hold (among them race, gender, and socioeconomic status) and the ways those identities can interact with weight stigma;
- Promoting intuitive eating and a pleasurable relationship with food, rather than external "eating plans" designed to shrink the body; and
- Supporting a joyful relationship with movement that allows people of all sizes, shapes, and abilities to determine their own level of engagement in physical activity.[25]

While approaches like HAES are helpful correctives to some of the trends we see in diet culture, there's still a long way to go. As a people plagued with brokenness and shame, we have a proclivity for setting up socially constructed hierarchies to assess the worth of others, to judge and evaluate their appearance, actions, and essentially their value as people. In the midst of our shame, our own self-criticism and harsh self-assessments overflow onto others. These assessments converge with others' judgments to create larger systems that herald some and marginalize others.

In America, we value those who are motivated, self-controlled, and disciplined, all of which are assumed of most who meet the slender physical ideal. So not only is thinness the benchmark for beauty in America, but it's become a reflection of favorable internal character as well. In this way, the value of thinness in our country is multi-layered—you're not only considered physically attractive but morally sound and personable to boot.

> Not only is thinness the benchmark for beauty in America, but it's become a reflection of favorable internal character as well.

Turning the Tide

At some undefinable moment during my time in intensive treatment, the whole backward nature of this judgment-based rating system for evaluating and respecting women sank in as never before. The ugliness and injustice of this socially constructed system settled within me in a new way as well. With fresh eyes, I noticed how both in subconscious and blatant ways, we treat certain people as more valuable based on their external appearance.

Not only did I realize that this system was morally wrong, but I saw how this socially concocted aesthetic hierarchy impacted the living hearts and minds of real women. I saw how it caused those not at the prestigious top wrung—as well as those who perceived they were not at the top—to feel pretty miserable. To intuit that you are not as respected as you should be because of the size and shape of your physically embodied self is a dismal reality.

These realizations were and are disturbing to me on a number of levels. For one, I don't believe our bodies were ever meant to be a statement about our internal character or worth. They're not meant to be an accessory advertising our appraised value to the world around us. Rather, they are a gift, the sacred dwelling place of our eternal souls. And every soul is invaluable.

I also reasoned that the same mysterious and loving God I had known my whole life might have something to say about this system of rating eternal souls. For years I had been familiar with the teaching that I was to love others as I loved myself,[26] and the beauty and profundity of those words came to light in a new way. I considered the widespread effects of what that kind of love, that kind of society, might actually look and feel like. In our own shame, brokenness, and self-criticism, we set up whole social hierarchies based on our judgment of others, which ironically begets more judgment, more shame, more ugliness.

I considered what it might be like to apply God's teaching on loving others in a new way. With regret and sadness, I recognized that I too had bought into this system of rating myself and others based on an external aesthetic. And I knew that was very much inconsistent with what God was inviting me to do. But now I was invited to see myself and others in an entirely different way. The only gaze through which I was to see myself and other people was one of love and compassion, envisioning my own and their unconditional worth. I was invited to offer myself and others a profound love that's not conditional on cultural standards or acceptance. I was invited to reflect a much greater love.

With admitted hesitation, I also realized that the linchpin in this whole system of judgment was how I viewed myself. The same eyes of judgment through which I viewed myself were the eyes through which I filtered my judgment of others. I was applying my own critical lens to those around me, whom I had very clearly been instructed to love. The way I viewed, loved, and valued myself directly affected my ability to love and value others.

In his usual air of wisdom, Richard Rohr articulates this self-other correspondence in the game of judgment:

> The way I viewed, loved, and valued myself directly affected my ability to love and value others.

As long as we are comparing and differentiating from the other, we can't love the other. We judge it. As soon as we are in a judging mode (higher/lower, superior/inferior) we can't love. . . . What flourishes is control, comparison, and competition—which blinds us to love.[27]

Essentially, a posture of love and a posture of judgment are in opposition to each other. A lens of judgment is antithetical to a lens of embrace, compassion, and love. They are contradictory postures of the heart and mind.

This correlation may seem glaringly obvious to others, but I had failed to recognize the incompatible nature of love and judgment. With new eyes I recognized that I could not love myself as God instructed me to do if I was constantly being harsh with, criticizing, or berating myself, *including about my external appearance*. I steadily recognized that my body was a very real, connected part of who I was. So I had to be compassionate with my whole self.

To the same point, I realized I couldn't love others if I was judging them. And to be completely honest, I was so entrenched in self-judgment that starting with the call to love others was easier than starting with relearning to love my whole self.

I was no doubt aware that self-love was part of the package, but that would mean giving up certain things the eating disorder had taught me to do, like expert self-criticism. I also knew that if I was to take God's words and instruction seriously—to adopt them in my head, heart, and actions—I had to change the way I viewed myself. I had to take a long, hard look at how I treated myself, at how I talked about myself, and at the internal self-talk I was using. In order to love others well, I also had to love myself well.

The only question I had was where to start.

FOR REFLECTION

1. "I had to take a long, hard look at how I treated myself, at how I talked about myself, and at the internal self-talk I was using. In order to love others well, I also had to love myself well." Have you considered this connection before? Is this something you've noticed in your own experience? How so?

2. (*For personal reflection, not necessarily to be shared aloud in a group.*)

   Take several minutes to sit with God in silence. Consider one or two of the most self-critical messages that emerge in your own self-talk (they could be related to your body or not). Notice what happens in your body as these messages come to mind. Is there a sinking in your stomach? Do you notice tension somewhere else in your body?

Now ask God to tell you the truth about these messages and how he sees you. Perhaps consult Scripture to help you come up with an alternative message about yourself based in self-compassion and love (see Zephaniah 3:17 and Psalm 139:1–18). Perhaps consider what a loving friend might say to you to counter these messages.

As you allow these messages to sink into your mind, also allow them to impact the rest of your body. Do you notice muscles relaxing or softening as you consider the gaze of love and truth teaching you new things about your worth? How deeply you are loved.

▌ FOR FURTHER STUDY

- Learn more about "Why Disordered Eating Is Everywhere" and the Health At Every Size approach from Dr. Jennifer Gaudiani, an eating disorders expert physician and the founder and medical director of the Gaudiani Clinic in Denver, Colorado, in episode 79 on the *Impossible Beauty* podcast.
- Learn more about "How God Sees Me" from bestselling author and the director of women's ministry at Ransomed Heart, Stasi Eldredge, in episode 25 on the *Impossible Beauty* podcast.
- Learn more about self-compassion from PhD candidate Marissa Knox in episode 15 of the *Impossible Beauty* podcast. In her research, Marissa focuses on exploring how

self-compassion acts as a source of resilience for healthy body image and stress management.

- Learn more about "Believing We're Beloved" from licensed professional counselor Aundi Kolber in episode 24 of the *Impossible Beauty* podcast. Aundi is also the author of *Try Softer: A Fresh Approach to Move Us out of Anxiety, Stress, and Survival Mode—and into a Life of Connection and Joy.*

PART 2

A JOURNEY OF
RESTORATION

7 HUMAN AGAIN

It takes courage to grow up and become who you really are.
—e. e. cummings

Hovering just beneath the surface of our everyday conscious awareness lie the contours of our deepest self. That which is most beautiful
within is, like a dynamic stream pulsing just below our awareness.
That which is within us is eternal.

Getting acquainted with our true self can seem elusive, likely because we're so often shrouded in layers of pretense and masks. Showing up as our true, vulnerable self often feels too exposing in a world
wrought with pain and criticism. So we abandon our inner voice and
deepest intuitions for the agenda or the roles the world around us
gives us credit for: looking perfect, being productive, making money,
and so on.

If these masks we wear are not the real thing, though, then what
makes up that dynamic, true eternal self? It could be said that it's the
purest form of who God created us to be. If we're each custom-made
by the most loving force we can imagine (even beyond what we can
imagine), if we're made in that image, then we likely manifest that
kind of beauty in varied and unique ways—as in at our core we are

uniquely beautiful and reflect the Life of God in profound yet distinct ways. Ways that only we can do.

Each of us is a limited edition.

So in real-life terms, you may wonder what it means to mine and search for the true self, that which we are intended and created to be. Practically speaking, I think the true self shows up in our varied personalities, preferences, passions, gifts, skills, and desires. For that reason, tools like personality assessments have helped me better understand and embrace who God has created me to be. To learn that I am introverted and intuitive and that I lead with my emotions and value order has allowed me to put words and logic to the reality I've lived out for years.

> Each of us is a limited edition.

Even more so, understanding myself as a Loyalist (six) on the Enneagram has enabled me to better understand and embrace my deep devotion to people and beliefs. This tool has also helped me accept and make strides toward befriending my core struggle with the anxiety and fear I so often come up against.

So these are all cognitive ways of describing myself, words and logic to describe certain dynamics of my personality, which I also believe are aspects of my true self. I'm also learning all the time how getting to know my true self is actually an embodied experience. It cannot simply be a cognitive exercise. As holistic beings, what we think about affects our emotions, and what happens emotionally affects us physically, and what affects us physically affects us spiritually.

In this way, our bodies are an integral part of the astounding human experience. Embracing the full experience of being human means embracing the gift of embodiment. We feel emotions in our bodies when we're devastated and our guts are hollow, or when we are anxious and our palms sweat. We experience passion in our bodies when our heartbeat quickens as we encounter a person or an experience that captures our heart.

We are a package deal, we humans: multidimensional, holistic, and interconnected beings. All our experiences and all we come to learn about our true self—in all of our nuances, passions, and persuasions—are filtered through every facet of the self: mind, body, and spirit. We know things cognitively, but we also experience the shape of our true self intuitively, in our physicality. Our bodily senses provide us with a wealth of information, and oftentimes our bodies know truth before our minds do.

All of that to say that the soul is eternal, and the soul is embodied.

Becoming acquainted with our true self becomes increasingly complicated when considering certain cultural baggage. In the wake of the influence of the philosopher Plato, the idea that the physical or material world is inferior to the mind and soul has been passed down to us, coloring the relationship we have with our bodies today. If we adopt the belief that our bodies are "less than" and essentially unimportant, it's difficult to honor our physical experiences and input in a meaningful way. This can lead to a significant split between the life of the mind and the life of the body.

This head-body divorce is even more exaggerated when considering the "never enough" voices associated with the American idea of beauty. Due to the flawless, thin ideal, so many women go about their life with body shame as their constant companion. They believe *they* will never be enough because they believe their bodies will never be enough in terms of meeting the cultural standard for beauty.

For these reasons and a host of others (including trauma histories such as physical or sexual abuse), many of us live our days as though we are a disembodied head. We deny and ignore the innate connection to our physical body, and so we live "cut off" from our embodied, physical reality. This is largely the case not only for women living under the yoke of cultural beauty, but as I became very familiar with, in the case of those experiencing an eating disorder as well.

Losing Touch

Somewhere in the course of adopting the ways of the eating disorder, this happened to me. I somehow lost touch with my true self, my own internal intuition and guide. You'd think by thirty-one I would have assuredly come into my own, or at least that's what movies, books, and my surrounding culture had led me to believe. But, no, there I was, shoulder-deep in food phobias and negative self-talk. Needless to say, my true self didn't get much airtime.

Though I didn't necessarily do much analytical thinking about my true self while in the trenches of intensive treatment, I do remember one afternoon when the reality of my own "out-of-touch-ness" with my true self became glaringly obvious.

We had just finished yet another therapeutic lunch and were doing our usual post-meal check-in. In that subterranean group dining room, one by one we debriefed around the table. I can't remember which brave woman was the first to say it as we sat there amid the empty plates, but she admitted that her meal had tasted good; she'd enjoyed it. Her bravery proved inspirational as a few other courageous women admitted that they too had enjoyed aspects of their lunch. I was one of them.

You may be wondering where's the story there. How is that in any way significant? But please understand, this is monumental. Having been swept up in and worn down by the currents of the toxic American beauty waters and the eating disorder, many of us at that Formica-topped table had convinced ourselves that food was bad because it equaled caloric intake. Food was no longer viewed as something to enjoy but a necessary evil, and the less food eaten the better.

Furthermore, the eating disorder tends to make rules against enjoying food, because if you enjoy it, you may eat more.

So year after year and meal after meal, the disorder can steadily erode any sort of pleasure that may be associated with eating. It hinges on this sort of adversarial relationship with food. And after years of this kind of thinking—food equals bad and hunger equals bad—physical cues such as the pangs of hunger or the discernment of food preferences can progressively wane.

Furthermore, hunger and enjoying food can easily become associated with shame, guilt, or moral weakness. You know, the kind of thinking associated with confessions like "Oh, I just couldn't help myself." So you learn to ignore those physical cues or vilify them, and soon enough, things get a bit out of sync. Essentially, you convince yourself that your body can't be a trusted source of information.

So there we were in the midst of this critical moment. The initial air of anxiety from which that first woman had spoken had subsided as others had joined her, and she was no longer alone in her bravery. We all sat there, quiet now, feeling a bit tentative about this new emerging relationship with food and what we'd just said.

The program therapist looked a bit stunned. She recognized the unusual nature of what she'd just heard, but after a moment of shocked silence, she stated she was grateful to bear witness to it. She explained that it was amazing to see how more life had been emerging from us as the eating disorder loosened its grip on us. As we were becoming more in touch with our bodies and its cues—our embodied experience— she noticed we'd begun to enjoy life more in its vast array of sights, touch, and tastes.

Then she thoughtfully paused before saying she hoped it didn't offend us by sharing it, but it was almost like we were "becoming more human."

After she spoke those words, my recognizing the "out-of-touchness" steadily sank in. It hadn't occurred to me how far I'd traveled from what I had once known so well—as in I didn't even know if something tasted good anymore. Amid the game of "never enough" and "never thin enough," the eating disorder had warped my mind and body to the point of not knowing simple food preferences or whether I was actually hungry. I had been lying to myself about what I liked and enjoyed in life, and it struck me as so messed up.

I was born to be fully human, to embrace life with my full self—body, mind, and spirit. And now I was angry that the disorder had taken from me some of the most basic elements of what it means to live life well and what it takes to embrace the true self God created me to embody. The ridiculousness of it all hit me in a new way. I had bought into the cultural demands for more miles and less food, and to what avail? To lose my soul, to lose my true self in the midst of it all?

As I'd pursued perfection, I'd lost myself.

The Awakening

As women, we so often numb out to our bodies because we feel shame toward them, or we numb out to our own internal voice, needs, or desires all in the pursuit of perfection: looking perfect, doing it all perfectly, having it all together, being the perfect friend and family member. We can also become numb to our own emotional experience so we can be there for others. But as we fail to be attentive to our own nuanced internal voice, perfection-based masks trump our authentic self. Our true self is drowned out by the drone of society's *shoulds* and perfectionism's *never enoughs*.

Admittedly, embracing and uncovering our true self is no quick or simple task. Getting acquainted with our authentic self is steady work throughout a lifetime. Furthermore, paraphrasing e. e. cummings, it takes courage to show up and be who we truly are. It takes awareness and it takes vulnerability, both of which require time, patience, and self-compassion to cultivate.

Despite the arduous nature of the work, nurturing our true self is the cornerstone to embracing the fullness of life for which we've been created. In order to embrace the richness and depth of who God has created us to be, we must be awakened to and aware of our full self: our unique thoughts, our diverse emotions, our physicality, our relating, our spirit. We must be aware of and attuned to the fullness of our experience, because that is how we embody our true self in the world.

The gift of embodied humanity allows us to embrace life in the fullness of our emotions, the fullness of our physicality, the fullness of our minds and our hearts. To run with abandon, to love others deeply, to embrace beauty, to serve wholeheartedly, to experience the love and leading of God. The great and tragic irony here is that the harder we run the race of pursuing cultural perfection, adopting all kinds of pretense, the less ourselves we become. The less human we become.

> The harder we run the race of pursuing cultural perfection, adopting all kinds of pretense, the less ourselves we become.

If we don't take notice of who we truly are and attend to how we show up in the world, the more we'll turn to the masks and pretense handed to us by our culture. We'll opt for whatever are the fashionable values, opinions, and preferences of the culture versus the voice of our God-given intuition and desire. We'll pursue perfection in the eyes of culture, because we don't know what else to aim for.

The problem with perfection, however, is that it's plastic. It's not lived in, it's not rugged, it's not real. Furthermore, as Richard Rohr so articulately states it, "The demand for the perfect is the greatest enemy of the good."[1] I would add that the demand for the perfect is one of the greatest enemies of the true self as well.

Rohr gives us some additional insight into the importance of awaking to the true self:

> We are given a span of years to discover [the true self], to choose it, and to live our own destiny to the full. If we do not, our True Self will never be offered again, in our own unique form. . . . Our soul's discovery is utterly crucial, momentous, and of pressing importance for each of us and for the world. We do not "make" or "create" our souls; we just "grow" them up. . . . We are charged to awaken, and much of the work of spirituality is learning how to stay out of the way of this rather natural growing and awakening. . . . We need to *unlearn* a lot, it seems, to get back to that foundational life.[2]

While perfection is a game of masks and pretense, embodying our true self is a sacred process of unveiling the unique beauty within us. And as Rohr explains, much of awakening to the true self is about unlearning and shedding that which is not life-giving. If the God in whose image we have been created is complete goodness, love, and light, then anything that doesn't reflect that within us is inconsistent with the eternal soul. It must be shed.

Interestingly, going through hard times and struggle is often when we're granted eyes to see our lives in greater perspective, causing us to cling to the things that truly matter. The real things. The eternal things. And so struggles refine us, leaving that which is lasting and eternal in their wake. In this way, developing what Rohr calls "our soul, our deepest identity, our True Self," is essentially playing the long game.[3] Pursuing goodness, beauty, and love doesn't change like the tides of cultural trends. We're developing and growing up into the deepest core of who we are and have been created to be.

And that core self is our eternal self.

Back to My Story

And so I set out on a journey to reclaim my true self. To *re*awaken to that which had been numbed within me, that which made me most human. I wanted to once again embrace the fullness of life and all the facets of who I was created to be. Food was no longer the enemy. My body was no longer the enemy. I was progressively seeing the eating disorder for what it was, for what it was taking from me. And so I fought back. And as I did, I steadily came back to life.

It was almost like becoming human again.

FOR REFLECTION

1. What do you think of the concept of the true self? Is this a new idea to you? Do you find it challenging, intriguing, inspiring, or something else—and why?

2. What are some of your favorite parts of who God created you to be? What character traits, personality traits, passions, skills, or interests do you really appreciate about yourself?

▌ FOR FURTHER STUDY

- Learn more about embodiment:
  - from licensed therapist and award-winning researcher specializing in embodiment, Dr. Hillary McBride, in her book *The Wisdom of Your Body: Finding Healing, Wholeness, and Connection through Embodied Living.*
  - from spiritual director Tara Owens in her book *Embracing the Body: Finding God in Our Flesh and Bone.*
  - Hillary was a guest on the *Impossible Beauty* podcast in episode 6 and Tara in episode 86.

8 THE BODY AS A MIRACLE

Self-rejection is the greatest enemy of the spiritual life because
it contradicts the sacred voice that calls us the "Beloved."
Being the Beloved expresses the core truth of our existence.
—*Henri Nouwen*

Your body is a miracle. *You* are a miracle. Without a doubt. From the
top of your head to your ten nimble toes, every last bit of you is sacred.

Just notice your breath. The rise and fall of your chest. The filling
of your lungs and the gentle exhale.

Now notice your next breath, and the next . . . and each steady
exhale. Each moment, each breath, is life. This gentle breath brings
life to every last corner of your embodied being.

Now feel your heart beat. And then beat again and again. Just think
about how many more times your heart will beat today, how it's been
steadily and faithfully beating—yesterday, last week, throughout your
lifetime. Each beat brings pulsating, dynamic life. Blood through your
veins and oxygen filling your lungs. This is what our bodies do for us
each moment of our lives.

Your body is a miracle, and considering the miracle of your body
may astound you. Your brain is made up of an estimated 100 billion
neurons,[1] your body an estimated 37.2 trillion cells.[2] The human body

is amazingly intricate and yet miraculously self-sustaining. Composed of numerous complex systems and sustained by a steady heartbeat, our bodies function decade after decade as though they're on auto-pilot. While the latest iPhone and Tesla car are dependent on being charged almost daily, the body is a self-sustaining miracle. During the course of our day, never do we have to tell our hearts to keep beating or our lungs to keep breathing.

So this is our reality each day, the reality of being human. We're given the gift of a functioning, living, complex and miraculous, breathing body. To embrace, dance, smell, taste, walk, skip. To take hold of the gift of life.

This was not my perspective a few short years ago. I likely would have affirmed that all those things are true, but it certainly wasn't the way I viewed or treated my body on a daily basis. The relationship I'd established with my embodied self was adversarial. I didn't trust my body. I believed it wasn't a reliable source of information.

Needless to say, the process of recognizing my embodied self as a miracle has been a bit of a process. In fact, recognizing the miracle that is my body happened very much in tandem with appreciating and embracing my physical self—essentially embracing the fullness of being embodied, of being human.

Breath as Life

That process of coming more fully alive as an embodied being, then, has in no way been instantaneous. Rather, reawakening to my essential humanity has been a bit clumsy and not at all linear. And that process has occurred in subtle shifts and waves. There was no burning bush moment, so to speak. No single bold or extraordinary event I can point to, like God's coming to Moses in the wilderness.

Instead, small "bushes" kept realigning me whenever I strayed from a course of healing. New insights I collected along the way gave me renewed hope to fight against the disorder, and then, progressively, my head, my body, and my heart worked in concert to steadily adopt a new way of being. Essentially, I had to entirely rework the way I viewed food, my body, and exercise, as well as how I treated and spoke to myself. So basically, a lot of things.

As someone who loved relationships and had built a career on studying and analyzing people's relationships with themselves, with others, and with God, I had somehow failed to realize that, like all of us, I had a relationship with my body. Even if I tried, I could never live fully as a disembodied head. Ironically, I also failed to see that, as with any other relationship, the way I viewed my body had to be cultivated and nurtured. Furthermore, establishing a helpful, life-giving relationship with my body—and with food—had to be worked at, particularly in a culture where I'd been inundated with skewed and unhelpful messages about all of the above.

> As with any other relationship, the way I viewed my body had to be cultivated and nurtured.

While so many things in the treatment environment worked together to shift the relationship I had with my body and with food, some of the most significant shifts in my recovery process that helped turn the tide happened in the midst of yoga, of all places. In that small basement yoga studio, filled with the intermingling scents of lavender and peppermint, is where that no small miracle happened.

Amid the everyday elements of yoga mats, essential oils, and casual active wear, something deep within me steadily shifted from self-scrutiny and judgment to self-acceptance and self-compassion. Furthermore, the adversarial relationship I'd once had with food and my body shifted to one of gratitude, grateful for the gift of embodied life and the gift of nourishment that sustained it.

It's also quite ironic that something about which I'd initially been skeptical became so transformational. Entering intensive treatment, I was nowhere close to a yogi, and I remember being confused about why yoga was even part of the treatment protocol. I just didn't see how it would in any way be helpful. I had done yoga here and there, but my experiences had spanned from somewhat relaxing to straight-up boring.

Furthermore, in a hurry to wrap up the whole intensive treatment thing ASAP and get on with my life, I viewed sitting in a dark room and relaxing as counterproductive. I wanted to get to the talking, the teaching, the healing. Basically, to *doing* something. Not sitting or lying on a mat as a potentially useful hour came and went.

Despite my resistance and overall poor attitude, however, I did yoga, and I did it often.

Then, some days into intensive treatment and well into my new routine of daily yoga, we had a substitute teacher. Like other yoga teachers I'd encountered, she too was a bit of a guru with her words. Early on in my new yoga career, I learned how yoga instructors often say these profound, multilayered truths about life to the point you wish you'd brought your journal along to write down their one-liners steeped in so much wisdom.

That day was no different.

There I was on my mat, the substitute teacher calmly guiding us through the practice. At some point she instructed us to simply lie down and notice our breath. I had been guided through this very same type of exercise before, but as she encouraged us to notice our breath and how it sustained our bodies, our being, the profundity of my breath became real to me. This breath gave me life, moment to moment. And the crazy part was that, as much as it kept me alive, I had never really noticed it nor been grateful for it.

The once-seemingly distant story of God breathing life into the first human in Genesis 2:7 became close and personal. The miracle and gift of breath became intimate. Sacred. "The man became a living being"[3] because of the breath of God. That suddenly felt true for me too.

My consciousness then spread out to think about all the other mind-boggling body processes happening in those moments, always working to keep my body alive. The miracle of my breath, the miracle of my body, sank in.

If that wasn't enough of a realization, the teacher then invited us to notice that our breath was a centering force that would always be with us, and the aha moment I was already immersed in went a little deeper. It occurred to me that just as the presence of my breath had been outside of my conscious awareness, the same was true in another sense. Because I was always so caught up in a list of *to-dos* and *shoulds* and what I believed I ought to do to please others and the world, I had failed to notice God in the present moment in any real or tangible way.

But, no, this breath, which I suddenly interpreted as God's presence—*his* breath—was always with me. And I could always center or be grounded in that presence. If I only had eyes to see it, so to speak.

So as I lay there on my mat that day, I became aware of the reality that the Life of God was pulsating in me and all around me. God's love, goodness, beauty, and Spirit were present with me and radiating from within me. The love I had theologized about, read about, learned about was traveling from my head to my lived experience as I envisioned the loving presence of God enveloping me.

It was decidedly a full-body experience, and as I continued to breathe deeply, my whole being relaxed as I settled more fully into the loving presence. This was an in-the-moment experience of God's grace. I usually notice his grace in hindsight, like, *Oh wow, in that hard situation, somehow things came together in a seemingly miraculous way.* But that day his grace wasn't a concept in my head but an in-real-time experience. God was very much with me in that moment. I was suddenly keenly aware of his grace, his love, his presence—that centering force I always have with me. All I had to do was simply open up my awareness.

That day shifted something in me. For years I'd been taught that God is always with me and all around me, but I'm not sure I associated experiencing the good things of God as an experience of God. Rather, I would secularize and normalize things like peace, joy, beauty, and grace, brushing them off as a good mood or good luck. But now I was able to connect the good things in life, like the peace I knew in those moments, as an experience of God. I became more aware of the fact that I was immersed in this life of peace and grace all the time; it was always swirling around me, beckoning me to embrace its beauty.

> This Life of God was so often revealing itself. I was just so often tuned out that I missed it.

This Life of God was so often revealing itself. I was just so often tuned out that I missed it.

The Rhythms of Self-Acceptance and Self-Compassion

Among the numerous gifts that came from experiencing God's grace and presence in such an embodied way was learning the rhythms of self-acceptance and self-compassion. As a bona fide people pleaser, I had the tendency to frantically run around like a chicken with its head cut off to be there for others, to try to look perfect, to try to be perfect.

The problem is these tendencies toward pursuing social acceptance and perfection had also somehow seeped into my relationship with God. Just as I felt about my acceptance by others, I truly felt

God's acceptance of me was dependent on what I did, so often wondering if I was enough. Quite honestly, I don't think I even realized I believed that, but my frantic and flurried actions revealed how fickle I assumed God's acceptance to be.

That's why that invitation to simply be still and breathe in the yoga studio was such magic. In a very real, tangible way, I could allow myself to let go. Let go of self-judgments and agendas. Let go of *shoulds*. Let go of perfect. And letting go in my body, allowing physical tension to be released, allowed me to settle into the present moment in a real way.

In the wholeness of who I was body, mind, and spirit, I wasn't striving but abiding. Abiding in stillness, peace, grace. And I didn't have to do anything to earn it or strive for it. It simply was.

So like all the rest, I learned that self-compassion is an embodied experience. As I settled into accepting and resting in God's grace, stillness, and peace, as I abided in these things, I found it easier to accept the fullness of who I was. Because the love of my creator was so palpable within and around me, it only made sense to internalize that grace and love. The reality that surrounded me assured me that I was entirely and perfectly loved; it was too strong a force to resist its truth.

> It's impossible to not love and accept yourself in the presence of Love itself.

Put another way, it's impossible to stand in the rain and not get wet. It's impossible to not love and accept yourself in the presence of Love itself.

And so I began to see myself with new eyes—as the daughter of the very author of life, of God himself. All of life's beauty and goodness are drawn up in his Life, and so, it stands to reason, there must be a good measure of that goodness and beauty within me. I just needed a little help to remember it was there.

And funny enough, the more I sat in that stillness in the following days and months, experiencing God's presence in the wholeness of who I was, the more I noticed it was more likely that God's Life, in all its loving-kindness, gentleness, and patience, would pour out from me and into the lives of others. God's compassion toward me allowed me to internalize that compassion toward myself, and I was then able to offer that compassion to others from an authentic, grounded place deep within me.

While shame had accused me of not being enough, God's grace and presence told me I was more than enough. Because of the depths he went to, I could touch and live in that grace. And I could rest easy in that.

Another Turning Point

In the days that immediately followed that day in yoga class, the wise words of the teacher and the idea that my body is a miracle unfurled within me. I began to consider my body in new ways, to respect it for what it can do and how it keeps me alive. How it's strong and allows me to do what I love. How without it, I could never embark on meaningful pursuits or beautiful adventures. All these realizations were a turning point for me in how I related to my body. I began to view it as a pivotal part of my whole self. I even began to trust it as a meaningful source of information. And that's a miracle in and of itself.

As my ability to trust my body increased, I also slowly learned to pay attention to its cues—all sorts of information about my emotions, my relationships, my spirit. A new wealth of information I had pressed the mute button on for so long was coming to life. It's as if I started to listen to an old friend who'd been whispering and sometimes shouting invaluable cues about my overall well-being. Befriending my body was like being invited into experiencing life in a whole new way. My whole self was invited to the party, a life in Technicolor, like Dorothy from *The Wizard of Oz* emerging from her black-and-white reality into the vibrant land of Oz for the first time.

So much life. And as I progressively spent less energy ignoring all the things my body was telling me, more energy was freed up to engage that life.

All this to say that, in an unexpected turn of events, yoga gave me a great gift, a gift I didn't even know I needed. The gift of awareness. With new eyes, I was awakened to the miracle of my life. I learned to trust and be grateful for the gift of my body. And I was awakened to the tangible presence of God.

Furthermore, as my mind stopped waging war against my body, food progressively became less of an enemy. Through yoga, therapy groups, and the wise words and kind patience of numerous therapists, I began to see food for what it truly is—the nourishment my body and brain need to live life well. As that ceasefire between my head and body settled into place, I was able to work toward an integrated view of my whole self, embracing the fullness of being human.

The Stifling

Looking back, I see how those seismic shifts could not have happened if I'd remained cut off to my embodied self. Beginning to befriend my body and welcome the gift of being embodied allowed me to embrace my physical self in increasing measure, along with my experience of God and the ability to better love my whole self. In order to embrace the fullness of my lived experience and the fullness of who I was, I could no longer ignore and deny my body.

Given that, on this side of that journey and with great clarity, I now see how the American idea of beauty stifles the gift of life and the miracle of our bodies. That system of valuing ourselves and others causes us to live with an unhelpful lens toward our bodies, and as a result, toward this life we're given. We're taught that our bodies are not vessels to create and live and love but commodities to be aesthetically refined and perfected.

American society has warped the way we relate to our bodies, teaching us to judge and scrutinize them rather than be grateful for them in all their life-giving and miraculous functioning. Magazines, commercials, and the media instruct us how to get rid of those love handles or that "stubborn belly fat," teaching us that certain aspects of a body are bad or undesirable and that we should seek them out and obsess about fixing them. This sort of rhetoric about correcting or improving our bodies has become so normalized in our society that it infiltrates women's coffee dates, shopping excursions, and casual chats. (Remember our discussion about Fat Talk.)

And all this convinces us American women that perfecting our external self is decidedly all-important, the definition of "arriving."

The way we're taught to view and relate to our bodies in our consumeristic society is a far cry from viewing them as miracles. And so our society is completely missing the point. It's entirely backward. As a marvel, the body is completely incompatible with the system that is American beauty. The body is not a commodity but a great gift. And logically speaking, a gift is not to be assessed and criticized but accepted and deeply valued. We're meant for so much more than critiquing the sacred vessel of our soul. We're meant to embrace it, thank it, and live out a life of meaning and purpose with it.

And so as I continue to journey forward in recovery and in our society, I desire to choose to see my body differently from how American culture daily tries to convince me to see it. And I desire that for you too. My hope is that, together, we learn to embrace the rhythms of self-compassion, gratitude for our embodied self, and the miracle of this life we're given.

▌ FOR REFLECTION

1. Have you ever considered your own relationship with your body? How would you currently describe that relationship?

2. How can we help cultivate and nurture the relationship we have with our bodies? What judgments about your body might be helpful to let go of in order to move toward this? (Feel free to keep this second question as individual reflection.)

3. Have you had an in-the-moment experience of God's beauty, grace, and love? If so, what was it like, and how did it impact you?

▌ FOR FURTHER STUDY

- Consider an intuitive eating approach to food. Intuitive eating is an example of tuning in to your body's cues versus following external messages from diet culture. Learn more about this approach to food by reading *Intuitive Eating: A Revolutionary Anti-Diet Approach* by Evelyn Tribole and Elyse Resch.

- Learn from author, survivor, and advocate Katherine Wolf about how "We Are All Miracles" on episode 51 of the *Impossible Beauty* podcast.

- Learn from author Jess Connolly about how "Your Body Is Not a Project" on episode 56 of the *Impossible Beauty* podcast.

9 REIMAGINING GOD

The people who know God well—the mystics, the hermits, those who risk everything to find God—always meet a lover, not a dictator. God is never found to be an abusive father or a tyrannical mother, but always a lover who is more than we dared hope for. —*Richard Rohr*

Reflecting back on the timeline for entering intensive treatment, I remember thinking how terribly inconvenient it was. I had been working toward full licensure as a marriage and family therapist for so long. For years. Graduate school, a nine-month practicum, hours and hours of client contact time, and I was almost done. So the idea of taking an intentional break so close to the finish line seemed a bit counterintuitive, even absurd.

Furthermore, I was just about to start graduate school round two. After practicing therapy for several years, I'd noticed how so many clients' desires and struggles seemed soul-deep, and the desire to meet people on a spiritual level grew within me. I had learned and developed the ability to come alongside others as they healed and connected within themselves and with other people, and I wanted to learn how to come alongside them in connecting with God as well. I had come to know God as the author of healing, and I desired to do my part in helping others connect with that true, authentic freedom that goes to the core.

And so I decided to take the unexpected path of pursuing a second master's degree, this time in spiritual formation. The only problem was that, as I began my first classes online, I was four months into intensive treatment and leaving it no time soon. In fact, I was going into a more intensive setting.

So after a lot of reflection and thoughtful conversations, I decided to press pause on my work as a therapist, and I was left with graduate school and intensive treatment, an unlikely pair. Though that mix seemed so strange and initially frustrating, I now see the gifts that came from it. As unhelpful beliefs, thoughts, and narratives eroded, more formidable ones were planted and taking root.

Furthermore, I was likely more perceptive than I might have been in other circumstances. Intensive treatment and all that comes with it is humbling. So truths that may otherwise have been glossed over or ignored, falling on deaf ears, instead became like lifelines to me. I scavenged for truth as the old things I knew—the old promises of perfectionism—showed themselves for what they were: empty.

> The old things I knew —the old promises of perfectionism—showed themselves for what they were: empty.

And so I went to intensive treatment programming during the day and came home in the evening to study, read, and write. During the day I steadily learned about and walked away from the deceptions and pretenses that didn't serve me. And at night I excavated and clung to the glimpses of life, truth, and beauty that emerged from my coursework. I read about the soul, the true self, the eroding effects of shame, the mystics' poetic love for God, and so much more. And as I did, my heart and mind steadily began to dwell more often on eternal things like God, love, goodness, and beauty, and less and less on self-judgments and criticism.

Don't get me wrong. I'm definitely no more spiritual than the next person. I wasn't drawn to these things because I'm any more religious than anyone else. Rather, certain situations seem to have the power to strip away what really doesn't matter in the end. Pretense and lesser things show their faces. Basically, I was unexpectedly being told that the way I was doing life wasn't working anymore. And the eating disorder wouldn't ease up nor could I reenter life as I had known it until some major things shifted.

All of that to say, when things get real, your perspective changes. And sometimes lesser things have to be done away with to make space for that which brings life.

The Reimagining

I admit it. I didn't give full disclosure at school. In online forums and in class papers, I identified myself as a marriage and family therapist. Which I was. Yet as you know, that didn't quite capture my nine to five commitments at the time. So at some points I felt like a bit of a fraud. Some of my new acquaintances had this faulty conception that if you're a therapist, you have it all together. Though I never think that's true, it felt especially untrue for me at the time.

You can imagine, then, my awkwardness and tentativeness when arriving for my first round of in-person intensive classes. I held the internal tension of wanting to be authentic with my new classmates while also not wanting to fall err to being that person who gives way too much information too soon. As a result, I was calculated about how much I disclosed and with whom. Being truthful about my struggles with food, exercise, and the like was new to me after being housed in the vaults of denial and avoidance for years, so imagining telling these practically strangers any piece of those struggles seemed unsafe and way too vulnerable.

But then it happened. The jig was up.

I was in a class on prayer when we were instructed to pair off, and the instructor explained that we were each going to pray for the other person. I internally cringed. My plan to avoid vulnerability seemed like it may be in jeopardy.

Just as my mind was scrambling, wondering what less vulnerable concern I could offer up for prayer, the woman sitting next to me glanced over. She looked friendly, and about ten years older than I was. Her eyes were kind, and she emoted a nurturing, maternal vibe. No words were exchanged. Only a rise of her eyebrows, basically asking, *Do you want to pair up?*

Well, I thought, *she seems pretty nice—and quite harmless.* Her glasses made her look studious too, like she'd be attentive. And her smile was soft and warm. Hurriedly, I assessed that she seemed like a good bet for a partner, but I may not tell her what I was really needing. What I was craving healing for.

Before I tell you what happened next, I confess that for years my struggle with an eating disorder and my relationship with God had seemed like they were on two parallel tracks. I just couldn't figure out what my faith had to do with my struggle with an eating disorder. Both had been steadfastly present in my life, but they failed to inform each other. Besides, I felt guilty knowing the tight grip the disorder's "rules" had on my time, thought life, and self-assessment, and I had this underlying assumption that God didn't like how fixated I was on exercise and eating "perfectly."

> For years, my struggle with an eating disorder and my relationship with God had seemed like they were on two parallel tracks.

In light of my uncertainty, I resolved to follow the rules of the disorder while simultaneously trying to follow the path I felt God was leading me on. I didn't like the fact that I couldn't integrate the two, but again, my faith felt separate from the disorder. And that was unsettling to sit with, to live with.

So back to my prayer partner. I'll call her Sarah, and as it turned out, she was all the things my gut had indicated she'd be. Of course, I let her go first; I hadn't yet decided if I was going to pray for the real thing or something less vulnerable I still hadn't come up with. So she shared what she wanted prayer for, and I prayed.

And to my surprise, in the space between Sarah and me, God spoke something deep and significant in the recesses of her heart. She was moved to tears.

Then it was the moment of truth. It was my turn to name what I wanted prayer for and time to decide how vulnerable I was willing to be. In a strange rush of courage and with a deep desire for God to speak into my decade-long struggle with food and all the rest, to speak to me the way he'd spoken to Sarah, I told her.

Not the extent of it. It was enough information, though, for her to come alongside me and ask God for some help. To speak a little light, a little truth into the shame that lingered in the cracks and corners of my struggle. The shame that said I wasn't enough who I was, that I had to strive and keep striving. That the only way I would be enough was if I attained perfection.

So there Sarah and I sat on a hard couch in a far corner of that satellite campus's sterile office building, me and this stranger-turned-prayer-partner. After she prayed for me, we sat in stillness. I was expectant. At times in the past, prayer had felt like talking into a formless void, like pouring my hopes, desires, and struggles into a black hole. So much poured out and nothing in return.

But that didn't happen now. There was no audible voice from heaven, but deep within me I had a steadfast sense that there was no need for striving. An inner peace and "settled-ness" accompanied that awareness, the message that I was enough. In that moment, nothing more could be done. Nothing more could be attained. Just as I was, in all my struggles and striving, in all my brokenness, I was loved. At my very core.

What came next was unexpected. For years I'd had an assumption that God was likely judging and critiquing me for the rigid and often obsessive way I related to food and exercise. In those moments with Sarah, however, those speculations were swept away. In the midst of prayer, she had artfully invited me to envision the face of God. Steadily, I allowed myself to go deep into my imagination. Allowing my mind to wander, envisioning what his face might look like.

I was surprised by what I saw. As I envisioned myself eye to eye with my creator, I noticed no sternness in his gaze, not an iota of judgment. Rather, his eyes were brimming with compassion. I was filled with a deep inner knowing that he understood. He had been with me the whole time. He'd not only borne witness to the struggles I'd been undergoing but understood it all so deeply. Every fiber of it. The empathy suddenly felt overwhelming.

I then sensed him assuring me, promising me, that he would help me. I wasn't in this alone. He was with me the whole way.

That experience shifted something within me. Call it wishful thinking or a figment of my imagination, but I'm certain it was neither of those. That experience was so unlike any previous experience I'd had. The soul-deep peace that accompanied those piercing truths was beyond anything my imagination had ever conjured or could ever conjure on its own. The realization that God was on my side, that he was with me shoulder-deep in the mess of it all, was monumental.

I think I'd truly believed I had to figure out all the anxieties and obsessions around food and exercise before I could go to God. That I had to get my act together, so to speak, in order to get back to growing spiritually. But now I realized that belief couldn't be further from the truth. In a new, very deep way, I experienced how God is an incarnational God. He comes into the messiness of being human and brings about healing, redemption, and light. He brings about hope.

In all my striving for perfection, inside and out, I think I'd been seeking some measure of control, seeking to alleviate the anxieties and uncertainties of everyday living. As I'd sought that control and pursued the cultural ideal, however, I'd put myself in an impossible situation, running after perfection on the proverbial hamster wheel—or again, down that rabbit trail—fueled by shame's taunts.

> The realization that God was on my side, that he was with me shoulder-deep in the mess of it all, was monumental.

The fact of the matter is I would never be enough on my own. I could never be perfect. As Richard Rohr says it, there is no "perfect" outside of mathematics and divinity. Furthermore, control and perfection could never give me the soul-deep acceptance I was longing for, the kind of soul-deep acceptance every human needs. Instead, rigidity and obsession became so loud in my heart and head that they easily drowned out the sacred interior whispers of God.

I was checking all the boxes but had lost the heart of things. What's more, somewhere in all that striving, I'd lost sight of the fact that God wanted to help me.

The Receiving

The best part about failing, about coming up dry, is that you're open to new ideas. When control fails, there's room for surrender. And surrender opens us up to God.

I think that's what happened that day with Sarah. My prayer with her was an act of surrender. That kind, practically a stranger, courageously came alongside me in prayer in a way I didn't even know I needed. I hadn't yet brought my struggle before God in such a raw and direct way as I did that day with her. Poised in a standoffish posture of control, I hadn't made space for him to come alongside me. I hadn't let down my guard enough and opened up my awareness to notice that, like a faithful parent, God was standing by, waiting for me to embrace the help he was so willing to give.

Furthermore, I hadn't realized that, the whole time, I'd had the antidote to shame with me, alongside me. Even dwelling in me. I simply needed to be awakened to his presence. I had forgotten, or perhaps never fully realized, that God was speaking over me and delighting in me all the time.

That whole concept of delighting in a person didn't fully come alive for me until my first goddaughter (and niece) was born. I hadn't experienced the miracle of creation that closely before. And I was there from the beginning. From the first time I held her, a tiny, intricate infant, until now as she's grown into a bright-eyed child, I can't get enough of her. Sometimes I just adoringly observe her; I can't wait to see what she'll do or say next. She's this astounding miracle to me, and I love every fiber of who she is and who she's becoming. Simply put, I delight in her.

I hadn't put it together in that way before. I hadn't considered how God had been there from the beginning for me too. And not just the beginning of my life on earth but from my conception, lovingly and uniquely weaving my very being together.[1] Considering and planning the unique beauty I would reflect in the world. From the beginning, he delighted and rejoiced over me.[2] And he still does. I had to strive for nothing. He gazed at me with more love and compassion than I could imagine. Just as I was. While trends of cultural beauty and acceptance would come and go, the devoted love and acceptance God had for me was eternal. Unchanging. And, of course, the same is true for you.

In all of this, I now realize that shame is so ominous because it first convinces us we're not enough, that we're wrong or bad at the core of who we are. We're then so easily lured by all sorts of empty things to run after in pursuit of somehow becoming good enough or good at all. For me it was perfectionism. For others, it may be achieving power or status or something else. Whatever it is, it results in chasing after what will not give us the life, the significance, and the acceptance our soul longs for. So while shame tells us we will never be enough, God's grace assures us that because of the outrageous love he has for us, we *are* enough.

That is the miracle of grace. And that is what our souls long for, what they were created to experience. That kind of unequivocal love and acceptance. And that is what God offers us. That is why God is our souls' true home.

And so that day with Sarah I saw with new eyes the advocate I'd had alongside me the whole time. The same God who created me, who had been alongside that naturally curly-haired girl as she grew up, was fighting for me and for the life of my true self. I suddenly became aware of how God—like Jane, like Eva, like my family and all the others who desired fullness of life for me—was alongside me. He was not judging me. He never was. He knew all too well the schemes of American beauty culture, of the eating disorder, of shame with its nefarious agenda, and all that they sought to diminish. But he had a life already purposed for me.

I became distinctly aware of the two very real pulls on my life, both battling for my affections and attention. One for life and goodness and one that would, if given the chance, ultimately lead to my destruction. In that battle, God wanted me to embrace the fullness of life for which I had been created in all its goodness and light. At my core, I wanted that too. I just hadn't realized I'd had such a powerful advocate at my side.

God was for me. And that changed everything.

| FOR REFLECTION

1. What do you find yourself running after to try to feel or become "good enough"?

2. What is it like to imagine God compassionately alongside you versus his being a critical outside observer? Does that fit with how you imagine God? Or do you envision something different? If so, what is that?

| FOR FURTHER STUDY

- Learn from spiritual director Elizabeth Peterson about "Engaging the Body in Spiritual Formation" in episode 98 on the *Impossible Beauty* podcast.
- Learn from licensed professional counselor Krispin Mayfield about "Connecting with 'the Invisible God'" and how our early-learned blueprints for relating impact our adult relationships and our relationship with God in episode 88 of the *Impossible Beauty* podcast.

10 REVERSING THE BABY SHOWER EFFECT

The loving relationship shared between Father, Son and Spirit is the ground on which all other models of life and creativity rest. In this relationship of constant self-giving, vulnerable and joyful love, shame has no oxygen to breathe.
—*Dr. Curt Thompson*

Crafting seems to be the trend. Crafting coffee or crafting beer. Essentially, spending a considerable amount of time on perfecting something. In similar fashion, we do this with our image. The image we want to project to the world. What we want the world to assume about us, to see about us, to know about us. I call it "image crafting"—only to myself, of course.

In so many pockets of American culture, image is everything. Advertising depends on it. We're sold all sorts of things with our assumption that they'll help mold our image. You are, for instance, rugged if you drive a Jeep or sensible if you drive a Prius. Certain personality traits or values are assumed of you by the image you hone and then portray to the world. And as we've already seen, this is also true of body image. Certain virtuous characteristics are married with a toned, thin figure.

All this image crafting has of course become even more exaggerated with the rise of social media. Now not only do we try to hone our image for our town's main street or our group of friends or co-workers, but for our hundreds or thousands of "friends" or followers online. There's just so much image maintenance to do. If we want the world to think we're funny, or carefree, or wise, or sexy, or dateable, or the perfect mom—or that we have the perfect home, family, or marriage—we have to craft that. By the tweets we tweet, the photos we post, the links we tag.

We spend so much time on our external selves. Wanting to look thin enough, fun enough, competent enough. We want others to believe this of us. We want to believe this of us too.

Given this is the culture we live in, the water we swim in, the air we breathe, this sort of image maintenance overtakes our female friendships. You know you've been there, during some event or outing with your female friends. At some point, someone mentions their recent exercise habits, dieting efforts, how "bad" they are for eating that dessert, or how great someone looks after losing the "baby weight."

(That's right, after the miracle of birth, as in a new human was created from almost nothing, we're going to focus on a mom's body image. After all her body has been through, all it's done. Do we ever pause to think about how backward that is? But I digress.)

Needless to say, so often what we talk about in our female group of friends is image-based. Where we're shopping for the clothes we wear, what cleanse we're doing, how cute that outfit someone's wearing is, how we really could stand to lose ten pounds—or how so-and-so could really stand to lose ten pounds. Furthermore, these groups often include a unique sort of posturing based on comparison to the thin ideal and then adherence to the diet and exercise habits that will get us (or someone else) to that ideal.

Simply put, the broken value system for women in America is often mirrored in our all-female groups, in our dialogue, and in how we compare and contrast ourselves with one another.

More than that, this value system often becomes amplified in these spaces, gaining significant momentum in all-female groups. Social psychologists call this effect *group polarization*, the phenomenon where people's individual decisions and beliefs become more extreme in a group setting.[1] And when cultural beauty narratives pick up momentum in all-female groups, I call that *the baby shower effect*.

I can't help but wonder if when we're doing this, allowing cultural values to overtake our friendships, we're totally missing out. What if our relationships could be so much richer, even healing? The way we relate with one another could be considerably deeper and more beautiful than the version our image-obsessed culture promotes. When we allow these cultural values to rule and navigate our relationships, we're playing it way too small.

A Bag Full of Rocks

I've had the same medium-sized, worn leather purse for the past seven years or so. So often it goes where I go, and it's become a time capsule of sorts. Despite my half-hearted efforts to clean it out, sorting through that purse is like sorting through the past seven years of my life. Scattered about at its bottom are a half dozen or so rocks. That's right. Rocks. When I went through security at a stadium venue for a concert last year, the security man scanned my purse, picked it up to hand back to me, and then with a smirk asked, "What do you got in there? Rocks?"

I smiled. I wanted to tell him, "Actually, yes. Good guess," but I didn't.

That probably sounds horribly illogical. Sure, the rocks are heavy, but they're not that heavy, and I can't seem to make myself take them out. I like keeping them where I'm reminded of them. You see, the rocks are significant because each one holds affirmations scrolled on them by the numerous women I journeyed alongside in intensive treatment. The tradition was this: each time you left a particular group, the remaining members gave you a rock. Each person wrote an affirming word or phrase, either a strength they wanted to call out in you or a wish they had for you.

Some may see those rocks for what they are on the surface—rocks with words on them. But I see them as so much more. You see, the honesty and intimacy that can occur in a treatment environment is intense. In those spaces, you're invited to speak the whole truth of who you are. And more often than not, people lead with their brokenness. There isn't much room or time for masks or pretense. Most women in our groups had reached some sort of rock bottom, and rock bottom has a way of weeding out pretense.

So in those groups, I got a crash course in vulnerability. As a therapist, I was used to inviting others to be vulnerable, but I hadn't realized how I'd lost those sacred spaces to practice vulnerability in my own life. When you try to be the one who's always there for others, it's all too easy to lose space to be broken yourself.

> When you try to be the one who's always there for others, it's all too easy to lose space to be broken yourself.

In those groups, I quickly learned I didn't have to be perfect. I didn't have to be the therapist, the fixer, or worry about saying the right thing. I had space to cry or get mad or just be in process. To be human. And there was so much freedom in that.

And as I was human and broken and entirely in process, my fellow group members did something amazing. They listened. As in they truly tried to understand and empathize with the heart of who I was and what I was saying. Among those women, I felt known. I was seen. My true self. Stripped of our masks and honest in our brokenness, we invited the fullness of who we were in all our strengths and weaknesses, beauty and brokenness.

And there, in those mostly sterile group rooms, among those Formica-topped tables and neutral-toned couches, something sacred was happening. In the midst of our "not enough-ness," we were not only known but accepted, the whole spectrum of who we were. And as we looked at one another, listened to one another, and loved one another, something deep within us was being healed.

The rawness that comes from shame's berating taunts telling you that you aren't enough is slowly eclipsed, slowly softened when you're reminded that you're loved. When you're loved right where you are and exactly as you are, you begin to believe there may be grace after all. And when others show you grace, somehow space is freed up to maybe be brave enough to extend some of that grace to yourself. To believe, even if for just a moment, that you are enough. And, in fact, perhaps you've been enough all along.

To speak our truth in a safe place. To be known. That's what we were created for. And that's exactly where shame is healed. When we're seen for who we truly are, when we're known even in our dark, shadowy places, and when we're loved.

At its core, shame taunts that because we aren't thin enough, pretty enough, competent enough, or whatever enough, we will be left. We will be deserted. Shame's ultimate threat is rejection and abandonment. While shame tells us who we are is bad, wrong, or not enough because of some brokenness or imperfection, grace counters that we are entirely loved in the midst of our brokenness. That is exactly what grace is. That is its beauty, its glory.

Some of the most important theology I've learned is that grace and love are embodied realities. You have to experience them to glimpse their power, to know their truth. You have to experience them to believe them. To look at someone in the midst of your "not enough-ness" and for them to return a gaze of love and compassion is love in the flesh. When we don't walk away from one another's brokenness but instead dig our heels in and stand next to one another when things are messy and entirely imperfect, that's when shame is healed. Grace leans in to hear the nuances of our story, attuning to the emotional subtleties in our face and in our demeanor. Seeking to understand and love.

Furthermore, to be vulnerable and your full self in those safe places takes great bravery. And it takes hope. Being brave enough to hope that when we show our more shadowy parts, we might receive grace in return.

Embodying love and grace to one another is so pivotal and so powerful because it reflects a greater love. When we really see one another and speak love over and into one another's lives and broken places, we're conduits of God's love. For that is how God comes alongside us. He truly sees us, knows us, understands our glories and our sufferings. And in it all, he loves. It is unceasing.

While shame threatens abandonment, God stands steadfast. He doesn't leave. His grace endures, accompanying us the whole time. And that too is where shame is healed—in the moments when we experience God in quiet, in our comings and goings, or in one another. When we recognize a gentle assurance that we are known and loved in those innermost places where shame once scoffed that we would never be enough. That's when shame is broken. When we know we're loved just as we are, reminded we are indeed enough, shame has no leg to stand on.

And so those half dozen or so rocks are a testament of true love and acceptance. Of what it's like to be known. And of my beloved-ness before God. Those women reminded me of the beauty of vulnerability and of true community. Those places where you can breathe deeply, show up in the fullness of who you are (in all your simultaneous splendor and messiness), be fully known, and be unequivocally loved. In those spaces we grow in strength and courage to embrace the fullness of who we were created to be. In those spaces we're reminded that we're not only broken but indeed manifest a beauty and brilliance in the world that is entirely unique and entirely sacred.

Soul Crafting—in Loving Community

So maybe this is how we take a stand against shame. Perhaps this is how we resist the villain's attempts to convince us that we're unworthy and will never be enough. I'm convinced that as women, we have a pivotal role to play in fighting against the system of American beauty. That system promotes shame within women and disintegrates female relationships, promoting all kinds of comparison and judgment in relationships that could instead be healing and so beautiful.

The system then goes a step further by making money on the fact that we don't think we're thin enough or young-looking enough or whatever enough—all the things American beauty culture just convinced us of. And again, we literally buy into our own exploitation, purchasing diet products, creams, or memberships to somehow be enough within that same broken system.

But what if we turned the tide in how we relate with one another as women? What if we opted out of the system of American beauty and instead related with one another in authentic love and grace?

> As women, we have a pivotal role to play in fighting against the system of American beauty.

My experience in intensive treatment gives me so much hope for this. Those models for vulnerable community developed in a matter of months, even weeks sometimes. Leading with humility rather than pretense. Somehow embracing that tension that we're indeed broken and need healing but that we also contain a sacred beauty within us that needs nurturing in safe community. And we called that forth in one another as we saw it.

I believe this is our charge as women. As groups of women. To be safe, loving places, rich with healing and encouragement. Places where we can speak the truth about what we see in one another, the truth of the beauty we see spilling over from our lives and hearts.

But none of this can happen if our relationships are so saturated with jealousy, with comparison, with judgment, all of which paralyze relational growth, health, and vulnerability. All of which are toxic to grace-filled, loving community. Yet that's the template for relating our culture gives us. The system of American beauty models and perpetuates comparison and competition among women, and such comparison breeds shame and relational brokenness.

In fact, on a neurobiological level, shame literally disintegrates within and between minds. Psychiatrist Dr. Curt Thompson, along with Dr. Dan Siegel, teaches that our brains function most optimally when they're integrated. They're most poised to support our mental, emotional, spiritual, and relational flourishing when their various domains are not only mature in their ability to do what they were designed to do but also able to fluidly communicate with the other domains.[2] When speaking on shame's effect on the brain, Thompson puts it this way: "The experience of shame disintegrates different neural networks and their corresponding functions within each individual brain."[3] Shame, then, literally disrupts neural connectivity.

Furthermore, the visceral experience of shame, the feeling we're "less-than" or not enough, also results in social isolation. Almost instinctively we move away from others when we feel we're not enough. As a result, shame has a disintegrating effect on community as well. When we're overwhelmed or even having a casual run-in with shame, our most basic instinct is to find the nearest rock to hide under.

Ironically, though, the hardest place to turn to is the very place that helps heal our shame—loving community. Thompson even discusses how moving toward safe connections actually reintegrates our minds. So while the shame-saturated system of American beauty has a disintegrating effect within and between us, feeling known and loved in safe and vulnerable communities heals shame. It literally heals, reintegrating our brains, restoring relationships. Comparison fractures while building one another up brings fullness of life.

And in loving community, we're not only known at our core but healed at our core.

So we have a good deal of agency in all this after all. Perhaps more than we assume. We often forget the power we hold. Real influence and say-so. What we do with our voice and in our relationships really matters. As women, we have a powerful role in fighting against our own exploitation based on how we relate with our female friends and acquaintances. We get to decide if we'll relate with them within the system of American beauty in a posture of judgment and comparison or from a place of grace and humility, leading with authenticity versus pretense, seeking to truly listen to and know them. Not because we might gain some status or improve our image, but because we're filled with and inspired by a greater love.

> In loving community, we're not only known at our core but healed at our core.

This is all so important, because just as shame has a spiritual gravity, beauty, goodness, and love do as well. And the more we relate with other women and within ourselves from a posture of love and grace, the more we feed the undercurrents of love and beauty in the world, diminishing the efforts of evil and its minion, shame. Again, the tenets of group polarization name how individuals' beliefs and actions become more extreme in a group setting.

Essentially, we have power to affect and influence one another. We have a voice that influences the groups we're a part of, and our groups influence the culture at large. The question is how we'll use the power we hold in those groups and friendships. Will we use our voice and our actions to further fuel the exploitative system of broken beauty? Or will we open wide the gates of grace, love, and vulnerability to create spaces that heal brokenness and shame?

So may we create something different in the world. May we curate sacred places where we are known and we know others. Where it's safe to be vulnerable, to be broken, and to show up in the fullness of who we are. May we be brave enough to speak of our brokenness and to nurture our true beauty. Brave enough to love others in their brokenness and have eyes to see and words to name the beauty we see in them.

Ultimately, may we find communities where we don't spend as much time crafting our image as time spent crafting our souls.

FOR REFLECTION

1. How might we move toward a culture of grace and love versus judgment and shame in our female friendships? How can we focus on soul crafting versus image crafting in these relationships?

2. In this chapter, I shared, "I was used to inviting others to be vulnerable, but I hadn't realized how I'd lost those sacred spaces to practice vulnerability in my own life."

142

- Have you experienced a relationship or space where you could be vulnerable, where you could feel known in your brokenness and seen for your unique beauty? If so, what was that experience like?

- Have you experienced grace during a season of brokenness? If so, what was that experience like?

- Do you have ideas on how and where you might seek that kind of space currently? (Perhaps if not in a friendship, with a therapist or spiritual director?)

FOR FURTHER STUDY

- Learn about our deep and fundamental human desire to be known, shame, and the healing power of community from psychiatrist, author, and speaker Dr. Curt Thompson on episode 33 of the *Impossible Beauty* podcast.

11 A NEW WAY TO DEFINE BEAUTY

I was created in love. For that reason nothing can express my beauty nor liberate me except love alone. —*Mechthild of Magdeburg*

The story of beauty is way bigger than what we imagine. I don't think we can even conceive of the fullness of beauty. Of what it truly is. While our culture associates beauty with attractiveness and thinness, I'm learning all the time how myopic that is. How very small that interpretation of beauty is.

Some of the most beautiful things I've experienced—sacrifice, friendship—are not skin-deep and are in no way based on aesthetic flawlessness. This includes wonders like the Grand Canyon or the stately Rockies.

Any glimpse into the majesty of nature is a lesson in the wildness and mystery that is beauty. Have you ever stood at the edge of the ocean, waves roaring, sea breeze tossing your hair, and though you squint to see it, you cannot conceive of where the water meets shore on the other side? It seems to go on forever. You feel so small. Or have you stared up at the clear night sky to see the countless stars staring back at you? So many. All at once you're overwhelmed. Simultaneously filled with the exhilaration of wonder and almost moved to tears.

I believe real beauty is eternal, and so things like love and sweeping seascapes are beautiful because they represent some sort of otherworldly quality, an eternal splendor. In those moments when we glimpse true, reckless beauty, our soul recognizes echoes of eternity, and we're met with a faint sense of heartache or longing. It feels like we were meant to know that kind of beauty, that kind of awe all the time. It's as if we were somehow made for limitless beauty, somehow made for eternity.

If it's true that beauty does indeed have an eternal quality, it stands to reason that true beauty may very well be bigger than any culture can define. Cultures throughout time have socially constructed what's deemed beautiful, slapping that label on what is considered attractive or aesthetically preferred. So when it comes to such cultural conceptions of beauty, they're often a fleeting and fickle notion, changing with the tides of fashion and marketing efforts. Cultural constructions of beauty are often only shadows or even imposters of the real thing, of a larger beauty.

Contrary to what the latest infomercial told you, there is no eternal glory in washboard abs or otherworldly splendor in the attainment of a flawless figure. While there's nothing innately wrong or bad about either of those, it's unhelpful to tout them as the quintessential linchpin for attaining beauty. So, you may ask, if being thin, young looking, and the perfect measure of "toned" don't represent the eternal gold standard for true beauty, what does, then? How are we to define or even begin to understand beauty?

What Is Beauty?

She was a hipster. Like, a real hipster.

She wore secondhand clothes, collected antiques, and was an artist for a living. She painted, mostly. Landscapes, not portraits. Her sense of fashion was diverse, and she donned it confidently, wearing a cropped leather jacket one day and an ankle-length wool pleated skirt the next. Her hair was blond, straight, and bobbed. Her eyes were steel blue.

She also played piano beautifully. During break times, she'd play the upright keyboard outside the group rooms, infusing the sterile treatment environment with a much-needed measure of elegance and transcendence. She was well rounded, gracefully stylish, and one hundred percent unique.

I'll call her Madeline.

One day when Madeline and I were part of the same psychoeducation group, when I was still in full-day programming, the topic was something like body image and the media. Somehow the group gravitated toward the topic of beauty in America, and suddenly I was so curious about this idea of beauty and how we've constructed its boundaries in American culture. How have we decided who's in and who's out? It all seemed a bit fickle and subjective in a way I hadn't considered before. So backward.

I wanted to know what the others thought about this idea of beauty that we've so myopically defined in our culture—that it's for the youthful-looking and trim women of America. So perhaps to the dismay of the group leader, I asked the group something like, "What do you all think beauty actually is? How would you define beauty?"

And then she said it. Just as you would expect a hipster guru to utter such a thing. So effortlessly, Madeline said, "Beauty is connection." It was as if I had pitched her the easiest question in the world and she'd been practicing that home run her whole life. *Oh*, I thought, *I've never really thought of it that way*. And to be totally honest, I wasn't completely sure what she meant. But it sounded so nice and she said it so confidently that I wanted to believe it.

The conversation moved forward, and others gave their input here and there. But I couldn't fully engage. I continued to sit with

Madeline's statement. The poetry and mystery of it intrigued me. I wanted to understand it, excavate it for its truth. Deep within me, I felt it was true, but I didn't know why. Looking back, I realize I could have simply asked a follow-up question. I'm sure she had a great explanation. I didn't, though.

> "Beauty as connection" felt like the trail of bread crumbs I needed to lead me on the path to deeper understanding.

In the end, perhaps it did me well to simply sit with her words, considering their truth and resonance in my mind and in my heart. In a way, the intrigue of Madeline's statement opened me up to considering beauty in a way I simply hadn't previously. It opened me up in such a way that I was able to take in a new conception of beauty I may not have if I hadn't been so hungry for a more grounded, steadfast understanding of what beauty was.

I could no longer sit with the broken, cultural version of beauty. I saw how it excluded people and perpetuated shame; how it brought about disintegration within and between people and relationships.

And those effects seemed anything but beautiful. The concept of beauty felt like it was on a higher plane than that. And "beauty as connection" felt like the trail of bread crumbs I needed to lead me on the path to deeper understanding.

Mud Pies

With his usual literary artistry, the brilliant British author and academic C. S. Lewis wrote,

> It would seem that Our Lord finds our desires not too strong, but too weak. We are half-hearted creatures, fooling about with drink

and sex and ambition when infinite joy is offered us, like an ignorant child who wants to go on making mud pies in a slum because he cannot imagine what is meant by the offer of a holiday at the sea. We are far too easily pleased.[1]

I can't help but wonder if it's the same with beauty, if our conception of beauty is way too small. If we are, in fact, missing out on a "holiday at the sea," essentially a conception of beauty that's far more encompassing, mysterious, and engaging than we ever imagined.

What if real beauty has everything to do with the Life of God and nothing to do with perfect skin or a toned physique? While the latter definition for beauty brings about shame and disintegration, embracing the former results in flourishing and joy—what I would expect to pour out from authentic beauty.

Embracing that sort of understanding of beauty, however, entails thinking about God in a certain way, perhaps even in a new way. A way that moves him beyond the static, stained-glass conceptions of God, from a God who not only *was* but to a God who *is*. The God who reveals himself in the Bible and the God who continues to act and reveal himself now, in this very moment.

Funny enough, my theology lesson in the dynamic God of the here and now came from an unlikely pair: a theologian named Baxter Kruger and a character named August Rush in the 2007 film by the same name. I was introduced to Kruger at about the same time I started my daily yoga practice in intensive treatment and began to embrace a more present-moment awareness of God.

It's as if Kruger puts words to what I was experiencing in a new way. In particular, he says the pulsating Life of God is unceasingly and dynamically present all the time and all around us everywhere—in the laughter of kids, in the love between friends and family, in the glory of sunflowers and sunrises. That life is essentially the active, eternal presence of God that always was, that is, and will be. That the energy of life is the love of God at work in the world. That the mysterious union and love between Father, Son, and Spirit are played out and revealed in all that is good, beautiful, and lovely. Kruger calls this abounding life and fellowship of Father, Son, and Spirit a great dance.[2]

Given that, I believe that when we experience or glimpse the dynamic Life of God in the world, we see beauty. It's as if true beauty is the evidence of his dynamic love at work, the ripple effect of his action. And so often that beauty is revealed in connection. Connection with creation, with one another, with God. And with ourselves, befriending and valuing ourselves, offering ourselves compassion.

And that is why we can see beauty in so many diverse places and interactions. Connections are everywhere. The Life of God is everywhere. We see it in nature, and we see it in relationships. There's this natural flow of connection, of life, of beauty. And as we're connected to God, we're freed from shame and enabled to befriend ourselves with grace. We're then able to connect with those around us via that same life and love we received from God. In the midst of a broken world, these are the cracks—the places we see heaven, or shalom, breaking in. Living. Moving. Being. Thriving.

So that is what I've come to. That is what I've concluded about beauty being connection. In this way, beauty is magnificent, and it's so big that it's hard to conceive of. The Life of God is mysterious. It can't be fully understood or contained, but it can be glimpsed. It can be experienced. And when we do take it in, we know beauty.

It's a matter of awareness. Seeing these connections. Seeing beauty.

Unfortunately, the shortsighted American version of beauty does us no favors. It makes beauty so small, so narrow, that our eyes don't see the expansiveness of beauty surrounding us every moment of our day. We miss the abundant Life of God abounding all around us because our eyes don't see the beauty outside the American brand.

And that's exactly what I love about August Rush. He's an elementary-aged orphan and musical prodigy who's well-versed in the art of awareness, of paying attention to the life all around us. "Listen," he says. "Can you hear it? The music. I can hear it everywhere. In the wind. In the air. In the light. It's all around us. All you have to do is open yourself up. All you have to do is listen."[3]

> We miss the abundant Life of God abounding all around us because our eyes don't see the beauty outside the American brand.

So may we have eyes and ears to see that music. May we have eyes and ears to embrace the Life of God all around us. May we know and may we embrace true beauty.

Not Mere Mortals

All of that to say this: What we think about beauty matters. How we define beauty matters. For one, it deeply affects how we relate to ourselves and to others. The interpersonal and intrapersonal effects here are massive. Do we see others through the lens of broken, cultural beauty? Or through an eternal view of beauty? Do we conceptualize beauty as reserved for the lean, youthful, and airbrushed? Or is beauty a wild and eternal force manifested in each one of us?

The American version of beauty implies that those who are "beautiful" are the ones who matter. They are the ones with social capital, who have a voice and are worthy of our respect. Yet an eternal view of beauty knows the secret. It knows there's more than meets the eye in all of us humans. We're not relating to mere mortals as we go about our daily lives. As we buy our coffee, ride the elevator, or do our work, we are in fact interacting with those created by and infused with the Life of God, endowed with eternal splendor and beauty.

We interact with one another so casually and nonchalantly that we easily forget we're dealing with those who image the creator of the universe. We so easily forget that about ourselves. Again, C. S. Lewis so artfully paints with words, this time what it might be like to glimpse the splendor of our fellow friends, coworkers, and acquaintances. Of *all* people. To consider for a moment what it is to be simultaneously human and made for eternity:

> It is a serious thing to live in a society of possible gods and god-desses, to remember that the dullest most uninteresting person you can talk to may one day be a creature which, if you saw it now, you would be strongly tempted to worship. . . . There are no *ordinary* people. You have never talked to a mere mortal. Nations, cultures, arts, civilisations—these are mortal, and their life is to ours as the life of a gnat. But it is immortals whom we joke with, work with, marry, snub, and exploit.[4]

So maybe the stakes are higher than we originally thought. Perhaps we and our other human counterparts are much more valuable and beautiful than we imagined. Simply because to be created is to be infinitely loved, meticulously formed, and beyond-our-imagination valued by the God of the cosmos. And if you have ever glimpsed any measure of the splendor and awe of nature, you can rest assured that the same creator lovingly and thoughtfully brought about an awe-inspiring creation in you. Your complex mind. Your heart. Your passions. Your gifts.

What if we took this eternal view of beauty seriously? What if we no longer viewed one another through the judgment-based "mud pie" version of beauty so prevalent in American culture? And what if we instead looked for and assumed the eternal splendor and innate beauty in one another and even within ourselves? What if we no longer viewed beauty as a derivative of a person's shape, size, or degree of aesthetic perfection and instead saw them through the lens of love and eternity? What if we chose to see the light of God in each person we encountered?

If we did opt out of culture's broken brand of beauty, I imagine shame and judgment would lose a great deal of airtime and that new pockets of love and compassion might be unearthed within us and between us. With shame and judgment effectively dislodged from our relationship with ourselves and with others, there may be even more room for more connection. For more real beauty.

> What if we chose to see the light of God in each person we encountered?

So may we aim for the brand of beauty that brings about flourishing and is grounded in love. May we have eyes to see the eternal beauty of each person we encounter, how each one uniquely reveals and reflects the beauty and mystery of God. How we reveal and reflect the beauty and mystery of God.

That's a new definition of beauty I can get on board with. The definition of true beauty. How about you?

▌ FOR REFLECTION

1. Feel free to grab a journal and, if you wish, a favorite drink. Then get comfortable and settle in. Take a few deep breaths and relax any places in your body where you notice tension. If it feels comfortable, sit up straight and feel how whatever you're sitting on is supporting you, how the floor is supporting your feet. Now take a minute or two to reflect back

over the past twenty-four hours or the past week, whichever is most helpful and accessible to you. I invite you to start noticing—and writing about if you'd like—where and when you experienced true beauty.

2. If possible, continue to sit in quiet. Take a couple more deep breaths, relax, and ask Jesus to show you the beauty of your own life.[5] Notice any images, emotions, words, phrases, or people that come to mind. Don't feel that you must force anything. Just notice what you notice.

▌ FOR FURTHER STUDY

- Learn about how to connect with our hearts and with God from therapist and bestselling author John Eldredge on episode 92 of the *Impossible Beauty* podcast.

12 RECOVERY AS RESISTANCE

The thief comes only to steal and kill and destroy; I have
come that they may have life, and have it to the full.
—*Jesus of Nazareth (John 10:10)*

For some, the villain's scheme shrouded in the American idea of
beauty is a distraction from fullness of life. For others, it paves the
way to their literal demise. In either case, it's a subtle and progressive undoing. A cunning ploy for the enemy of our souls to deplete
and destroy us.

Before I extend the invitation I believe God offers us all, let's briefly
review the two core realities I believe we as women must grasp before
we can recover from the push and pull of American beauty culture—
realities we need to fully understand in order to effectively resist
them.

1. We're Being Played

Under the shame-saturated reign of cultural beauty, our worth and
acceptance become conditional on meeting the ever-changing, largely
unrealistic standard for beauty in America. And again, under this
reign, it's the goal and the agenda of advertisers and marketing executives to convince women that we're not good enough, thin enough,

perfect enough. Aesthetic perfection in America is a moving target and unrealistically proportioned on purpose.

I invite you to remember Paul Hamburg's words: "The media markets desire. And by reproducing ideals that are absurdly out of line with what real bodies really do look like . . . the media perpetuates a market for frustration and disappointment. Its customers will never disappear."[1] The more we can be convinced we aren't good enough, we don't look good enough, we aren't fit enough, our food isn't perfect enough, or we aren't whatever enough, the more likely it is that we'll buy some product, supplement, or service to perpetually strive for the current version of beauty. And the more we strive, the more money advertisers and marketing executives make on us.

Our shame is highly profitable to the powers that be in the systems of American beauty and to the villain himself. This cannot be emphasized enough: We're being played.

2. Shame-Based Striving Brings Disintegration and Disconnection

In the midst of all our "never enough" shame-based striving comes all sorts of disintegration and disconnection. Here are two broad categories of those harmful effects:

We live a burdensome life of judgment toward ourselves and others.

As shame makes itself at home in our lives, and the cultural brand of beauty becomes our measuring stick for success, worth, and acceptance, we use that measuring stick for ourselves and for others. And with each judgment, we become more disconnected from ourselves and others. We move away from love and compassion and toward judgment and condescension. Other women become a means for comparison and objects to be evaluated. We relate to one another based on an assessment of our external shells versus our internal beings.

Intriguingly, I think we've also been taught that we're doing ourselves a favor by being so critical toward ourselves and our bodies. I personally had somehow settled into the belief that the stricter I was with myself, the better. The more my inner critic resembled a drill sergeant, reminding me of popular culture's rules around food and exercise, the better. The drill sergeant didn't care if I was tired; I had to go another mile. The drill sergeant didn't care if I was still hungry, because diet culture had taught me to watch my caloric intake like a hawk.

And somewhere in all this self-judgment, condescension toward any perceived aesthetic imperfection and harshness toward our bodies in general, we lose something so central and so sacred. I know I did. So often when we're convinced that our body doesn't quite measure up, we disconnect from it. And in that process, we disconnect from all its wisdom, from all our internal intuitions and instincts.

But those instincts help us recognize things like physical fatigue and pangs of hunger, and those deep intuitions within us are the voice of our true self.

We cut ourselves off from not just our bodies
but from our true self and God.

When we don't pay attention to the subtle shifts and cues of our internal world, we essentially cut ourselves off from the very cues that make up the voice of our true self. How do we know our values, our passions, or our gut instinct unless we tune in to the holistic cues of our bodies and being? Furthermore, when we reject our physical selves, we tend to cut ourselves off from the still, small voice of God within us, or at least limit our experience of it. Yet we've been created to experience God in all of our fullness—mind, body, and spirit.

And when we don't integrate our physical selves into that experience, we may miss out on the subtle whispers of God that teach us more about who he is and who he has created us to be. Where do we find joy in life? What makes us laugh? What awakens compassion within us? How do we know unless we pay attention to our *whole* selves?

> We have been created to experience God in all of our fullness—mind, body, and spirit.

And, again, shame literally disintegrates neural networks, the same neural networks that help support our holistic thriving when they're connected. For when our brains are integrated, we're best poised to relate with ourselves and others more thoughtfully and less reactively.

Shame disconnects at every level, then—within our brains, in how we relate to ourselves, in how we relate with others, and within our communities. Put another way, shame takes us further away from the shalom reality we've been created for, to thrive in.

And so embracing the American idea of beauty is a useless chasing of the wind, a relentless ride on a hamster wheel, a fruitless race down a rabbit trail. It is not good for us. It is not good for our souls. It charades in so many forms, but its root is shame and striving.

There is a better way.

An Invitation to True Beauty

Let me present a more beautiful picture for you instead—a steadfast journey toward wholeness and true connection.

The same Dr. Curt Thompson I've quoted so often in this book explains that "[God] is transforming us—creating us anew—to re-commission us to do the work of new creation along with him."[2] Put another way, our purpose in the world is to be deeply connected with God, continually transformed and renewed by him so we might also create good and beautiful things alongside him.

We have a pivotal role to play in the story of redemption and re-creation in the world. *You* have a pivotal role to play in the story of redemption and re-creation in the world.

Thompson goes on to explain that "God's intention for us to bear his image as co-creators is truncated by the great payload of shame we find ourselves managing. In doing so, we burn so much energy that we are rendered unable to create in the ways envisioned by God."[3]

What we do with our lives matters. What we do with beauty matters. We've been created to make artifacts of beauty in the world and in our lives. Shame, however, takes up the sacred energy we have to put toward creating more beauty in the world. Christy Harrison says something similar about diet culture, a system that thrives on the fertile ground of shame: "It keeps us too hungry, too fixated on our bodies, and too caught up in the minutiae of our eating regimens to focus our energies on changing the world."[4]

Thus, Harrison and Thompson would agree that shame, in its many forms, gets in the way of our fulfilling our good and beautiful purposes in the world. To engage life that is truly life. Shame is a colossal distraction; shame breeds colossal distractions. In this way, the story of shame and so the story of American beauty are anything but beautiful. They work against beauty in so many ways. Shame is beauty's nemesis.

Shame does not have the last word, however. The story of true beauty is steadily at work in the world as well. Just outside our distracted awareness is a sacred rhythm, an eternal stream of life in our midst. The life and action of God played out among us, streams of connection, goodness, and splendor flowing and emerging around us and within us.

What I love about this story, about this particular understanding of beauty, is that it's invitational, because the Life of God is invitational. We are personally invited to join the story of beauty. Our creator, who lovingly knit us together, reaches out his hand, inviting us to join him in bringing about beauty and redemption in a broken world. In making all things new. In this way, beauty is way bigger than we had imagined, and we are welcomed into it.

> Our creator, who lovingly knit us together, reaches out his hand, inviting us to join him in bringing about beauty and redemption.

To understand this invitation to beauty in its fullness, we must return to the book of Genesis—location, the garden of Eden. There God's original intention for humanity was realized, a reality in which humanity was intimately connected to God, to one another, and to creation. Literally, it was the garden of delight. A reality where shalom reigned.

Despite the disintegrating and disconnecting effects of sin that came about there, however, God was and is so in love with his creation that he is a tireless seeker of restoration. Of restoring that original connection with us so we may restore our interconnection with him, ourselves, and others. God's essence is unity and love, and we are ultimately and continually invited into that reality.

We know beauty is at work in the world when we see its fruits— wherever we see redemption, goodness, and love. Though we don't currently see God in a tangible, human form, we see him in the shape of beauty at work. We experience him in our intimate relationships where we are seen, known, and loved. Where our shame is healed. Our brains are reintegrated.

In this way, beauty is not a removed, impersonal reality or a rigid, perfect aesthetic standard. It's more like a dance, the dynamic Life of God played out all around us. A dance of redemption, of bringing beauty from brokenness, of making all things new. And again, we're invited to participate.

And this is the part I love, where our true self finds its place, where it realizes its unique meaning in the world. Where we realize that we are indeed a part of something much bigger than ourselves. We are a part of the Life of beauty itself. In all our quirkiness and giftedness, personality and even struggles, we're grafted into this larger mission of redemption. In all of our individuality, we each have a pivotal part to play in the unfolding story of beauty. As light shines through a prism, we reflect the love and beauty and character of God in our unique ways, in our unique being.

Simply put, the voice of the true self and our role in the story of beauty is manifested in our creativity. Wherever we're working to bring about new things in the world through art, or writing, or cooking, or hosting, or loving, we're essentially working alongside God to bring about more wholeness, beauty, and goodness. In all our creative endeavors, we're coming alongside him to make the world a more beautiful, loving, and good place. To join the streams of goodness and love that bring us closer to God's original vision for his creation in the garden of Eden, where humanity was wholly connected to our creator, ourselves, one another, and the creation.

For we become most wholly ourselves when our soul is connected to God and infused with his life. That life is then expressed in the unique creativity that flows out of us. In this way, the voice of the true self and our connection with God are very much interdependent.

So as we embark on creative endeavors—in all our making, loving, and doing—it is indeed the Life of God working through us. Our unique presence and creative expression are founded in our true self and are an overflow of our connection to the life and love of our creator.

And that's why it's so pivotal to embrace our true self and not some carbon copy our culture endorses. As Richard Rohr puts it, "We must find out what part of the mystery it is ours to reflect. There is a unique truth that our lives alone can reflect. That's the only true meaning of heroism as far as I can see. . . . Our first job is to see correctly who we are, and then to act on it."[5] As limited editions, so to speak, we have unique ways to manifest beauty in the world. We are made in the image of a God who is making all things new, and we are invited to work alongside him to do the same.

Of course, shame will no doubt arise at points in the journey of the true self. It will warn against vulnerability and embracing the fullness of who we are. And American beauty will try to distract us from the voice of the true self, endorsing a fixation on some sort of aesthetic flawlessness or the means to achieving such flawlessness. Indeed, if we are so distracted by the shame-saturated currents of American beauty, we'll be hard pressed to attune our hearts to the eternal undercurrents of authentic beauty. But those undercurrents are so important. They are where the voice of our creator speaks in our inmost places, leading us to embrace the fullness of his love and the contours of our true self.

And if we are truly in the midst of a saga of beauty versus shame or good versus evil, we should not be surprised by tactics that distract us from realizing our true identity. For if we do take hold of that identity, manifesting new things in the world alongside God, we will no doubt bring about new pockets and reflections of beauty. Shame will lose its stronghold as the reign of true beauty expands.

The Larger Beauty

I want to make one last point about the saga of beauty in our midst, and that is to mention what we're working toward.

Have you ever noticed the bittersweet nature of experiencing authentic beauty in the world? Or how beauty can somehow feel otherworldly? How true beauty has such a captivating quality, and how somehow it simultaneously causes your heart to ache a bit? As if your heart desires to experience even more of that beauty in all its fullness? It's as if our hearts were made to forever bask in that kind of splendor.

I've come to believe that we are in fact a part of that larger beauty. Our hearts were created to experience it in all its fullness. So in those moments of awe and wonder, our hearts bear witness to our soul's true home. An eternal home, where that kind of joy and authentic beauty is as abundant as the air we breathe. For if God is ultimate, unfiltered beauty and we have been created for intimate connection with him, it only stands to reason, then, that we are most at home in his presence. In the presence of Beauty himself.

And that is exactly what the story of beauty teaches. God is tirelessly working to reestablish a reality in which all his children are connected to and caught up in his love and beauty. In this saga, God is after our hearts, for us to know the depths of our "enough-ness" in his embrace. As children find their home with their parents, so we find our home in connection with our creator. Shame's back is broken when the creator of the universe and the author of eternity lavishes us with love and unconditional acceptance, claiming that we are indeed enough.

And that in his love, we always have been.

The Resistance

So, again, there you have it. Two counterforces at work in the world: the currents of beauty and the currents of shame. The former filled with thriving, connection, and wholeness, the latter with disintegration and disconnection. A classic conclusion would be to say that it's our decision which one we choose to follow—which wolf we choose to feed, as the adage goes.

Yet in the case of American beauty, I'm not sure it's that simple. As we've learned, shame is crafty. The messages associated with American beauty are so sneaky that we often don't even know we've bought into them. I don't think many of us even realize that we've adopted this shame-based system of striving that tells us our value is in our thinness. Simply put, as we learned from pastor Greg Boyd, you can't get out of a cage you don't know you're in. And that's exactly why I hope you now see the truth of American beauty. That you now see the sneakiness uncovered to reveal its nefarious motives that seek to convince us we aren't enough.

So by all means feel free to care about your nutrition. Eat nutrient-rich foods, because they fuel your body and your brain and because your body is a gift. And may eating not be an occasion for obsession or being punitive but an opportunity for gratitude. And feel free to move your body. Run, jump, swim, or dance. But please don't do it because your Fitbit requires more steps that day or because magazines exhort you to be beach ready for swimsuit season. Move, laugh, be present, and enjoy your body, because you have been given life. And because each breath you're given for that life is a miracle.

All of that to say, now that you know the cage that is American beauty, I invite you to opt out of it. To opt out of what strips you of true life and to opt in to something greater. To fight against this system's shame-saturated motives and villainous agendas. To opt out not only because of its harmful, diminishing, and disintegrating effects but because of what it holds you back from and gets in the way of. You are a sacred being, an embodied soul created to be connected to and caught up in the Life that is God. A life of connection, a life of creativity.

That is the fullness of life for which we are created, and so that is where we find joy and meaning. Seeking life outside that connection will come up empty and dry, I assure you.

So how do we practically resist the shame-based messages of broken beauty that say we're not enough? How do we combat the shame-based striving to always do more or be more—essentially, to be perfect? I'll tell you how. Trust in the voice of grace. The loving reality of God that surrounds you and is in you. God's grace is not just a nice idea but a living reality. It presses in on you and delights over you. It is real. It is strong.

> God's grace is not just a nice idea but a living reality. It presses in on you and delights over you.

It is eternal. And it has the final word, not shame, and certainly not the broken system of American beauty that says your worth lies in how thin or toned your body is.

My Ongoing Journey

You may be curious about where I am in all of this now, how I'm doing in my own resistance against the system of American beauty and even the eating disorder. Well, these days I'm no longer sitting at Formica-topped tables, and my battle is less with beef stroganoff and pizza and more with noticing the voice of shame. I'm aware of its shape-shifting nature, and I'm learning to look out for its taunts that say whatever I'm doing is not enough. In my battle against shame, I've found some of my best weapons to be self-compassion and gratitude. Being gentle with myself. Knowing that I can do the best I can in life *and* that I am human. I try to discern what my role is in a life season, a situation, or a relationship, and then seek to trust God with the rest.

I'm not perfect, nor do I want to be. Perfection is not possible, nor is striving for it fun or human. I'm not called to be perfect or to do it all, only to be faithful in what God is asking me to do.

I've also learned the wisdom of vulnerability. Vulnerability can be hard, and it often comes with practice, but that's where richness and healing happen. When I allow myself to be vulnerable, to show my imperfections and struggles, I open myself up to be fully known. Only when I open up in the midst of trusted others or before God can I be healed and held in my deepest places and struggles.

I'm also trying to show up for my own life. To live my own story. Not just listen to others, trying to help them from the sidelines. Helping others can be a beautiful thing, but the action of God is alive in my own story, and it serves me well to be attentive to that.

In my battle against shame and American beauty, a vital weapon has also been reconnecting to my body through yoga, slowing down enough to realize that each breath is a gift. And recognizing the love and acceptance of God in real time with each breath. Like, right now. Knowing that love and acceptance are real and all around me. I'm immersed in them all day, every day. And as I'm more connected with my physical self, I'm also more grateful for my body and the food that nourishes it. I recognize my body as a gift, food as a gift, and movement as a gift.

And, last, as I journey forward, I try to do so from a stance of "daring greatly" as Brené Brown would put it, or in Richard Rohr language, trying to live from the center of my true self. To do that, though, I have to pay attention to my thoughts, my heart, my emotions, my body, because that's where the voice of the true self and the voice of God speak. I also have to be brave, because oftentimes what arises from my authentic, vulnerable self may be not cool, trendy, or popular. But it is what's true within me. Then to act on that truth or speak that truth often takes great bravery as well.

All of that to say the journey of resisting the system and the disorder that claims that my worth is in the size or shape of my body isn't easy. It's a process, and it's a group of daily commitments. But these days it's feeling less and less like a battle and more and more like a new way of life. Thankfully.

These commitments are to self-compassion, non-judgment, practicing gratitude, thanking God for food and for my body, being mindful of God's loving presence, and always remembering the voice of grace that has the final word. I am loved and accepted, with no conditions, right now and always.

Soul-Deep Beauty

That's my story. The story of how the gravity of American beauty took over my life for a bit. How it ran the show for a span of years. How it took over aspects of my true self and the passions and pursuits for which I was created.

But sometimes the best part about life making you pause is how that pause changes you. How it causes you to reassess and redirect because what you're doing simply isn't working anymore. To notice what is no longer bringing life and find a new way forward.

Amid that pause, I realized the tremendous sway American beauty has over the minds and hearts of so many women. How it has co-opted the head and heart space of countless others, not just me. So much time and energy is spent striving to be enough, thin enough, perfect enough. Wanting to look slim in that selfie or for that wedding. I saw how that whole system for assessing women's worth is broken and fleeting. How it diminishes women's true life, true identity, and true self. I saw how that system had diminished my own life, and I wanted something better for other women too.

I was also introduced to and inundated with the depth of a new kind of beauty. The beauty of God's life at work in us and among us, and that's changed the game. Life is no longer as small as abs and perfection but as expansive as galaxies and a grace I don't understand.

A kind of beauty that blows my mind and seems too good to be true. But it's that kind of seemingly impossible, soul-deep beauty I'm trying to learn the rhythms of and become more immersed in every day. It's that kind of beauty that's worth my time, my energy, my life.

And so, again, I invite you to join me in opting out of the system of American beauty and into the story of true beauty. To opt out of the small game of culture and into the expansive game of eternity. To resist the undercurrents of shame and to settle into the embrace of grace.

May you know that your worth is not tied up in your size or shape or the flawlessness of your skin or body. That your life is so much bigger than that. That a very real and loving God surrounds you and sings over you. The author of life says you are entirely enough and always have been. You've been made for so much more, for an entirely greater kind of beauty. An authentic, enduring, and even eternal beauty.

May you be freed from the brokenness and diminishment of shame so you can take your place in the unfolding story of beauty.

May you—may we—be freed to image the God of creativity, who is making all things new and bringing about true beauty in the world.

| FOR REFLECTION

1. In this final chapter, I've named what's been helpful in my journey of walking away from cultural beauty and toward true beauty. Do you connect with any of the following (or from the additional takeaways from other chapters) that could be helpful in your own journey? (As well, is there anything I don't talk about that you've found to be instrumental in walking away from American beauty and embracing true beauty?)

- In chapters 1 and 2, I discuss the helpfulness of media literacy or looking at media and advertising with a critical eye, asking questions like, *What am I being sold here? What is the story I'm being asked to believe?* Also, *Is someone trying to make money off my shame or my not feeling good enough, or causing me to strive after a moving target of beauty or perfection?* Naming these things and noticing these trends helped me extricate myself from the shame that comes from such messaging and images.

- In chapter 4, I discuss how shame is a minion of evil seeking to deplete and diminish humanity at every turn and divert our mission of redemption and unity, co-creating good and beautiful things alongside our creator. I realized that fighting against shame, American beauty, and the eating disorder was fighting against the villain, the enemy "that comes only to steal and kill and destroy."[6] That changed everything.

- Here are some excerpts from this final chapter:

> "In my battle against shame, I've found some of my best weapons to be self-compassion and gratitude. Being gentle with myself. Knowing that I can do the best I can in life *and* that I am human. I try to discern what my role is in a life season, a situation, or a relationship and then seek to trust God with the rest."

> "I've also learned the wisdom of vulnerability. Vulnerability can be hard, and it often comes with practice, but that's where richness and healing happen. When I allow myself to be vulnerable, to show my imperfections and struggles, I open myself up to be fully known.

Only when I open up in the midst of trusted others or before God can I be healed and held in my deepest places and struggles."

"A vital weapon has also been reconnecting to my body through yoga, slowing down enough to realize that each breath is a gift. And recognizing the love and acceptance of God in real time with each breath. Like, right now. Knowing that love and acceptance are real and all around me. I'm immersed in them all day, every day. And as I'm more connected with my physical self, I'm also more grateful for my body and the food that nourishes it. I recognize my body as a gift, food as a gift, and movement as a gift."

"As I journey forward, I try to do so from a stance of 'daring greatly' as Brené Brown would put it, or in Richard Rohr language, trying to live from the center of my true self. To do that, though, I have to pay attention to my thoughts, my heart, my emotions, my body, because that's where the voice of the true self and the voice of God speak."

". . . always remembering the voice of grace that has the final word. I am loved and accepted, with no conditions, right now and always."

"I was also introduced to and inundated with the depth of a new kind of beauty. The beauty of God's life at work in us and among us, and that's changed the game. . . . A kind of beauty that blows my mind and seems too good to be true. But it's that kind of seemingly impossible, soul-deep beauty I'm trying to learn the rhythms of and become more immersed in every day. It's that kind of beauty that's worth my time, my energy, my life."

2. (*For individual reflection and practice*)

Again, Brené Brown defines shame as "the intensely painful feeling or experience of believing that we are flawed and therefore unworthy of love and belonging."[7] When considering the topics of food, body image, or beauty, do you notice shame arising in relation to any particular belief, thought, or aspect of this conversation? If so, bring this shame out of hiding. Perhaps spend some time asking God where or with whom you can share this. (A therapist? A spiritual director? A close friend or two?) Is God inviting you to sit quietly in prayer with him, waiting for a word, phrase, or image from him?

Notice where you feel that shame in your body. Is it a sinking feeling in your stomach? Tension in your shoulders? Where does the shame live? Next, ask God for an image of his love and grace. Perhaps sunlight or rain. Picture God's love and grace saturating those areas of tension in your body where shame is showing up. Just sit in that grace, allowing it to do its work. Notice if anything emerges as you sit in this grace—a word, phrase, image, or something else.

3. What is one artifact of beauty you feel God is inviting you to make or continue making? (This could be relational, artistic, creative, or anything simple or not that serves to bring more goodness, love, and beauty into the world.)

_____

_____

_____

4. After reading this book, have you noticed any shifts in your ideas around beauty? If so, please name them.

_____

_____

_____

5. What is one thing you want to take with you from reading this book? What action step(s) can you take in light of this shift or takeaway? Take ten minutes to sit with God and write an action plan for going forward.

    Examples:

  • Make an appointment with a therapist or anti-diet dietitian to further explore your relationship with food, your body, and movement.

  • Identify unhelpful cultural messages you're believing/telling yourself regarding beauty or body image (e.g., "Thinner is better," "I will be happy when . . ." "The more exercise, the better," "The less food, the better," "My food must be 'perfect'"). Consider what more helpful, balanced thinking might look like. Also consider talking to a therapist about these messages and beliefs.

- Become more familiar with diet culture messages and consider an anti-diet approach. (I've found Christy Harrison's *Food Psych* podcast to be very helpful with this.)
- Become more familiar with intuitive eating.
- Consider your family culture regarding food and body image. Is it helpful? Could some shifts be made to move away from shame, diet culture, or judgment?
- Consider not labeling foods as good or bad.
- Practice not judging or commenting on the size or shape of people's bodies.
- Read one of the books recommended for further study, such as *Breaking Free from Body Shame* by Jess Connolly; *The Wisdom of Your Body* by Dr. Hillary McBride; *Intuitive Eating* by Evelyn Tribole and Elyse Resch; *How to Raise an Intuitive Eater* by Sumner Brooks and Amee Severson; *Anti-Diet* by Christy Harrison; or *Mothers, Daughters, and Body Image* by Dr. Hillary McBride.
- Learn more about media literacy and how to be a critical/mindful consumer of media.
- Explore a Health at Every Size approach.
- Reduce your time on social media.
- Unfollow social media accounts that don't build you up.
- Consider following accounts that demonstrate body diversity.
- After determining what such a practice would look like, engage in a daily or weekly prayer time that reminds you of God's tangible love for you.
- Talk with a friend or two about changing how you talk about food and your bodies.

- Plan a regular mindful walk, noticing beauty in your surroundings.
- Practice seeing true beauty in the world and in people around you.

▌ FOR FURTHER STUDY

- To learn more about healing from shame in communities and partnering with God to create beauty, check out Dr. Curt Thompson's book *The Soul of Desire: Discovering the Neuroscience of Longing, Beauty, and Community.*

A THREE-DAY
RETREAT GUIDE

Dear Reader,

I have experienced the difference between information and transformation, and it's my deepest hope and prayer that the content of this book won't simply be more information for you but an opportunity for God to do a deeper work in your life. New insights, healing, and vulnerability most often come when they're given time and space to emerge. And that's why I'm extending an invitation to engage in this three-day retreat experience with a friend or two or a small group of friends. Also, please note that the facilitator role is quite casual—mostly requiring only someone open to guiding your group through the questions and that's about it.

I am so excited and grateful for the work God will do in your groups, and I wish you much fruitful and healing dialogue. May you feel loved and known by God and one another.

Melissa

Opening prayer (optional):

We open our lives to you today, God. You have knit us together and know everything about us, and you love us deeply, more than we can imagine. You want us to heal; you want us to thrive. If there are any places in our lives where we could find more freedom, please bring that to light. If there are places where you want to open us to truth, please soften our minds and hearts to be open to what you want to speak to us. In the days ahead, may we find healing, and may we come away knowing you more. May we experience your love deeply and know in our deepest places, in our essence, that you are beautiful. May you bring healing, truth, and help to places of brokenness or shame. We pray for healing.

Questions for Reflection

(Note to facilitator: Either use all the questions below or select the ones that seem most fitting for your group and time format. Also, feel free to offer any of the questions below as a writing prompt only or a write-and-then-respond prompt. Again, whatever feels best for your group.)

1. In chapter 2, Melissa says, "I awoke to how women are valued in America and in the world, and I didn't like it. I also began to see the real-life implications of that value system. I noticed how it affected the women around me physically, mentally, and spiritually." Have you noticed this value system for females? If so, how do you see it impacting girls and women?

2. So often our high expectations for ourselves or perfectionism strengthen the voice of the inner critic. Is there an area of your life where you notice that happening? Perhaps an area where you could invite more balance or self-compassion to enter in?

3. Learn from renowned advocate and author Jean Kilbourne in this TedTalk (suggested clip: 0:00-7:18): https://www.youtube.com/watch?v=Uy8yLaoWybk.

   What do you find interesting or surprising about this clip? Does anything stand out to you?

4. In this clip, Jean Kilbourne says, "So our girls are getting the message today so young that they have to be incredibly thin, and beautiful, and hot, and sexy, and that they'll never measure up to this impossible ideal." Is this something you've noticed as well? How so?

5. Media literacy is "the ability or skills to critically analyze for accuracy, credibility, or evidence of bias the content created and consumed in various media, including radio and television, the internet, and social media."[1] In other words, media literacy is to thoughtfully assess media, often for persuasion. When viewing media, social media, or advertising, helpful questions might be:

   • Is someone trying to sell me something?

   • What is the implied message here or what is the implied message someone is trying to convince me of? (If I buy *x*, I'll be happy or more socially acceptable.)

   • Is this image real? What has been retouched here? What body parts have been dramatically reduced or enhanced?

   • How might media literacy help disarm cultural messaging around beauty and thinness?

6. Where are you seeing "perfection" sold these days (social media, media, advertising)? What emotions come up for you when you encounter these images?

7. "Shame sells" (chapter 3). Have you found this to be true? How does this statement strike you?

8. In chapter 4, Melissa writes, "We've become so entrapped by American standards for beauty and the lifestyle associated with that standard that unhelpful and even harmful behaviors and beliefs regarding food, exercise, and body image are normalized." Have you noticed any unhelpful yet normalized beliefs regarding food, exercise, and body image? If so, what are they? Have these beliefs impacted you? If so, how so?

9. Also in chapter 4, Melissa says, "The problem of epidemic negative body image and eating disorders in America is not strictly a physical problem; it's a problem that penetrates every layer of our being. It's a problem that is psychological, emotional, and assuredly spiritual." How might unhelpful cultural beliefs around beauty and body image impact a person's overall well-being (physical, thought life, emotional, relational, spiritual)?

Wrap-up question for day one: What is one thing you want to take away from today's discussion?

DAY 2: BROKEN BEAUTY BREAKS US
(CHAPTERS 5–8)

(Note to the facilitator: This day has been broken into two sessions in case you would like to leave space between sessions for participants to eat lunch,

go for a walk, or engage in some other contemplative or rejuvenating activity. Again, feel free to do what is best and most fitting for your group.)

1. Brené Brown defines shame as the "intensely painful feeling or experience of believing that we are flawed and therefore unworthy of love and belonging."[2] What is it like to consider shame as "a minion of evil"? Can you think of any ways shame might "fracture our soul's well-being, our unity with others, and connection with our creator"?

2. In chapter 5, Melissa expounds on how "shame is a minion of evil" and seeks to deplete and diminish humanity at every turn, diverting the mission of redemption and unity, co-creating good and beautiful things alongside God. Melissa states this realization was a turning point for her. Fighting against shame, American beauty, and the eating disorder was fighting against the villain, or the enemy "that comes only to steal and kill and destroy."[3] How does this idea sit with you? Is this something you've considered before? Does this strike you as a helpful idea?

3. In chapter 6, Melissa writes, "I had to take a long, hard look at how I treated myself, at how I talked about myself, and at the internal self-talk I was using. In order to love others well, I also had to love myself well." Have you considered this connection before? Is this something you've noticed in your own experience? How so?

4. *(For personal reflection, not necessarily to be shared aloud in a group. The recommendation for this practice is 10 to 30 minutes.)*

   Take several minutes to sit with God in silence. Consider one or two of the most self-critical messages that emerge in your own self-talk (they could be related to your body or not). Notice what happens in your body as these messages come to mind. Is there sinking in your stomach? Do you notice tension somewhere else?

Now ask God to tell you the truth about these messages and how he sees you. Perhaps consult Scripture to help you come up with an alternative message about yourself, based in self-compassion and love (see Zephaniah 3:17 and Psalm 139:1–18). Perhaps consider what a loving friend or relative might say to you to counter these messages. What do their eyes, face, or smile look like as they communicate love, acceptance, and delight? As you allow these messages to sink into your head, also allow them to impact your body. Do you notice muscles relaxing or softening as you consider the gaze of love and truth teaching you new things about your worth? How deeply you are loved.

(Suggested break time)

5. In chapter 7, Melissa says, "It could be said that it's [the true self] the purest form of who God created us to be." What do you think of the concept of the true self? Is this a new idea to you? Do you find it challenging, intriguing, inspiring, or something else? And why?

6. *(For individual writing and reflection. Participants can share after individual reflection and writing if they'd like.)*

   What are some of your favorite parts of who God created you to be? What character traits, personality traits, passions, skills, or interests do you really appreciate about yourself?

7. *(For individual writing and reflection. Participants can share after individual reflection and writing if they'd like.)*

Have you ever considered your own relationship with food or your body? How would you currently describe the relationship you have with food and/or your body?

8. (*Have participants write or reflect on this question individually.*) In chapter 7, Melissa shares, "Ironically, I also failed to see that, as with any other relationship, the way I viewed my body had to be cultivated and nurtured. Furthermore, establishing a helpful, life-giving relationship with my body—and with food—had to be worked at, particularly in a culture where I'd been inundated with skewed and unhelpful messages about all of the above." How can we help cultivate and nurture the relationship we have with food and our bodies? What judgments about food or your body might be helpful to let go of in order to move toward this?

9. Have you had an in-the-moment experience of God's beauty, grace, or love? If so, what was it like, and how did it impact you?

Practice: A Letter to Your Body

Researcher, author, and therapist Hillary McBride says, "If you have an experience of your body as good, it will be easier to think of your body as good."[4] Write a letter to your body as if she were your closest friend. Suggestion: Begin with apologizing ("Dear body, I'm sorry for . . ."), move to what you appreciate about your body, and then move into celebration ("I loved when we went for that hike . . .")

- Stay with the good. Practice treating your body as a being that is worthy of honor and respect.[5]

Wrap-up question for day two: Do you notice any shifts that have occurred in your thoughts or experience regarding beauty, your body, or something else?

▌ DAY THREE: WE CAN CHOOSE SOMETHING DIFFERENT (CHAPTERS 9–12)

Practice: "Full Body Prayer" from Tara Owens's book *Embracing the Body*

(Note to facilitator: Guide participants by reading this prayer/practice aloud.)

Start by sitting quietly and acknowledging God's presence and provision in prayer and thank him for the gift of your body. Close your eyes [if you'd like] and breathe deeply, noticing your breath going in and coming out. Don't try to stop all your thoughts . . . just let them pass by you without interacting with them or mulling them over . . .

Begin [by] paying attention to your feet. Flex your toes and roll your ankles. Notice any tension, pain, pleasure, any sensations in particular that come to the forefront. Don't worry if there's nothing dramatic or obvious—just keep your awareness there . . .

[Now] begin noticing your legs, then knees, then hips. What sensations are housed there? Is there anything pooled or collected in any place in your joints or muscles? Do you feel any shame or a specific awareness of these parts of your body? . . . Keep breathing deeply, imagining the flow of air—the breath of God—moving into the places that you've turned your awareness to. Is there anything here that feels different or worth noting? Tightness? Openness? Move your attention up to your waist, then stomach, then low back, staying for a while in each of these places and noticing any sense of connection or disconnection, any numbness or life speaking in these parts of you.

Then bring your awareness to your chest and shoulders. Roll them gently if you need to—most of us hold a great deal of tension here. What do you feel as you pay attention to this part of your body? What's the predominant emotion or sensation? Before moving up to your neck, face, scalp, take some time to notice your arms, wrists, and hands. Bend your elbows and rotate your wrists. Curl your hands into fists and then flex them out into open palms. Wiggle your fingers and feel the joints move. Are there any clear sensations lodged in your upper body? What feelings are being carried in the palms of your hands?

Finally, rotate your neck slowly and move your facial muscles any way that feels natural to you. Our faces both hold and express a great deal of our emotions—many of them we haven't taken the time and attention to be aware of. Is your jaw tight or clenched? Do you feel able to move it and feel openness? What about your throat? Is it relaxed and elongated, or clogged with unspoken thoughts? Notice the muscles of your cheeks and eyebrows, the feelings around your eyes. Do you feel sensation or emotions there or in the top of your head? What does this slow noticing of your body's main command center bring to your attention?

Before you come back to your surroundings, spend a few minutes appreciating the grace of your body. It may not work the way you most deeply hope, and it may not be molded the way you would like, but it is who you are. You are this flesh and blood and muscle and bone that you've been contemplating for these minutes, and the essence of who you are is embedded in every cell. Express gratitude to God, as you can, for the gift that is your embodied soul, unique in every way.

When you're ready to return to your surroundings, spend some time thinking about the sensations and emotions you noticed in various places within you. The sadness that you felt in your . . . [stomach], the sort of empty oddness that resided there—can you put a name to it? Does it have a color or a word associated with it? Don't try to force things, but notice if it has anything to say to you. If you feel stuck, turn to God and ask him if he has anything to reveal about this place in your body and what he might be communicating through it to you. This flesh of ours is an incredible gift, and the sensations we feel in and through it carry wisdom and grace to us. The simple fact that we are being physically renewed—we have a physiologically new body every seven years as each cell dies and is replaced with new life—speaks of God's care, kindness, and attention to our bodies.[6]

Take a few more deep breaths. Open your eyes and come back into the room as you're ready.

(*Note to facilitator: Please leave time for participants to share what it was like to engage in this practice.*)

Questions for Reflection

(*Note to facilitator: Again, feel free to dwell on the questions where your group feels most drawn. Reflect on or discuss any or all the following questions based on your group's needs.*)

1. In chapter 9, Melissa writes, "I now realize that shame is so ominous because it first convinces us we're not enough, that we're 'wrong' or 'bad' at the core of who we are. We're then so easily lured by all sorts of empty things to run after in pursuit of somehow becoming good enough or good at all."

   (*Note to facilitator: Give participants the option to write or reflect on this question individually if preferred.*)

   What do you find yourself running after to try to feel or become "good enough"?

2. Also in chapter 9, Melissa reflects on her realization that God is on her side. What is it like to imagine God compassionately alongside you versus a critical outside observer? Does that fit with how you imagine God, or do you envision something different? If so, what is that something different?

3. How might we move toward a culture of grace and love versus judgment and shame (and comparison)—in our female

friendships in particular? How can we focus on soul crafting versus image crafting in these relationships?

4. In chapter 10, Melissa shares, "I was used to inviting others to be vulnerable, but I hadn't realized how I'd lost those sacred spaces to practice vulnerability in my own life."

   - Have you experienced relationships or spaces where you could be vulnerable, where you could feel known in your brokenness and seen for your unique beauty? What was that experience like?

   - Do you have ideas for how or where you might seek that out currently? What are they? Perhaps if not in a friendship, with a therapist or spiritual director?

Practice: Noticing True Beauty

1. Get comfortable. Feel free to grab a journal and a warm drink, and settle in. Take a few deep breaths and relax any places in your body where you notice tension. If it feels comfortable, sit up straight and feel how whatever you're sitting on is supporting you, how the floor is supporting your feet.

   Now take a minute or two to reflect over the past twenty-four hours or the past week, whichever is most helpful or accessible to you. Start noticing, and writing about if you'd like, where or when you experienced true beauty (in people, places, experiences, interactions, provision, and so on).

2. If possible, continue to sit in quiet. Take a couple more deep breaths, relax, and ask Jesus to show you the beauty of your own life.[7] Notice any images, emotions, words, phrases, or people that come to mind. Don't feel that you must force anything. Just notice what you notice.

3. In the final chapter, Melissa names what has been helpful in her journey of walking away from cultural beauty and toward true beauty. Do you connect with any of the excerpts below from the final chapter (or the additional takeaways from other chapters) that could be helpful in your own journey? Is there anything Melissa doesn't talk about that you have found to be instrumental in walking away from American beauty and embracing true beauty?

   (*Note to facilitator: Give participants several minutes to look over the following bullet points and reflect before sharing with the group.*)

- In chapters 1 and 2, I discuss the helpfulness of media literacy or looking at media and advertising with a critical eye, asking questions like *What am I being sold here? What is the story I'm being asked to believe?* Also, *Is someone trying to make money off my shame or my not feeling good enough, or causing me to strive after a moving target of beauty or perfection?* Naming these things and noticing these trends helped me extricate myself from the shame that comes from such messaging and images.

- In chapter 4, Melissa discusses how shame is a minion of evil, seeking to deplete and diminish humanity at every turn and divert their mission of redemption and unity, co-creating good and beautiful things alongside their creator. She realized that fighting against shame, American beauty, and the eating disorder was fighting against the villain, the enemy "that comes only to steal and kill and destroy."[8] That changed everything.

- In the final chapter, Melissa shares, "In my battle against shame, I've found some of my best weapons to be self-compassion and gratitude. Being gentle with myself. Knowing that I can do the best I can in life *and* that I am human. I try to discern what my role is in a life season, a situation, or a relationship and then seek to trust God with the rest."

- Also in the final chapter, Melissa writes, "I've also learned the wisdom of vulnerability. Vulnerability can be hard, and it often comes with practice, but that's where richness and healing happen. When I allow myself to be vulnerable, to show my imperfections and struggles, I open myself up to be fully known. Only when I open up in the midst of trusted others or before God can I be healed and held in my deepest places and struggles."

- As well in the final chapter, Melissa says, "A vital weapon has also been reconnecting to my body through yoga, slowing down enough to realize that each breath is a gift. And recognizing the love and acceptance of God in real time with each breath. Like, right now. Knowing that love and acceptance are real and all around me. I'm immersed in them all day, every day. And as I'm more connected with my physical self, I'm also more grateful for my body and the food that nourishes it. I recognize my body as a gift, food as a gift, and movement as a gift."

- "As I journey forward," Melissa shares, "I try to do so from a stance of 'daring greatly' as Brené Brown would put it, or in Richard Rohr language, trying to live from the center of my true self. To do that, though, I have to pay attention to my thoughts, my heart, my emotions, my body, because that's where the voice of the true self and the voice of God speak."

- Last, from the final chapter, Melissa says, "I was also introduced to and inundated with the depth of a new kind of beauty. The beauty of God's life at work in us and among us, and that's changed the game. . . . A kind of beauty that blows my mind and seems too good to be true. But it's that kind of seemingly impossible, soul-deep beauty I'm trying to learn the rhythms of and become more immersed in every day. It's that kind of beauty that's worth my time, my energy, my life."

Practice: "Walking with God" (based on a practice developed by Tara Owens[9])

"Take thirty minutes . . . to go for a walk with God. . . . Leave the things that might distract you (mobile devices, mental to-do lists) [behind]. . . . Take a deep breath as you step out the door, and pray these words: *Jesus Christ, I commit this journey to you. I want to walk with you, God. Let me feel, see, and know what you would have for me in this time."*[10]

Here are potential ideas for reflection and prayer as you walk. (If you prefer to sit versus walk, that is of course great as well.)

- Idea #1: Do nothing. After all that has been contemplated and discussed these past couple of days, see where your mind leads you. What is still sitting with you? What ideas, images, or words is God bringing to mind? What might God be inviting you to do going forward—or not do?
- Idea #2: Brené Brown defines shame as "the intensely painful feeling or experience of believing that we are flawed and therefore unworthy of love and belonging." When considering the topics of food, body image, or beauty, do you notice shame arising in relation to any particular belief, thought, or aspect of this conversation? If so, bring this shame out of hiding. Perhaps spend some time asking God where or with whom you can share this. A therapist? A spiritual director? A close friend

or two? Is God inviting you to sit quietly in prayer with him, waiting for a word, phrase, or image from him?

Notice where you feel that shame in your body. Is it a sinking feeling in your stomach? Tension in your shoulders? Where does the shame live in your body? Next, ask God for an image of his love and grace. Perhaps sunlight or rain. Picture God's love and grace saturating those areas of tension in your body where shame is showing up. Just dwell in that grace, allowing it to do its work. Notice if anything emerges as you sit in this grace: a word, phrase, image, or something else.

Final Questions for Reflection

1. After reading this book, have you noticed any shifts in your ideas around beauty? If so, name them.

2. What is one thing you want to take with you from reading this book? What action step(s) can you take in light of this shift or takeaway? Take ten minutes to sit with God and write an action plan for going forward. Examples:

   • Make an appointment with a therapist or anti-diet dietitian to further explore your relationship with food, your body, and movement.

   • Identify unhelpful cultural messages you're believing/ telling yourself regarding beauty or body image ("Thinner is better," "I will be happy when," "The more exercise, the better," "The less food, the better," "My food must be 'perfect'"). Consider what more helpful, balanced thinking might look like. Also, consider talking to a therapist about these messages and beliefs.

- Become more familiar with diet culture messages and consider an anti-diet approach. (Melissa has found Christy Harrison's *Food Psych* podcast to be very helpful with this.)
- Become more familiar with intuitive eating.
- Consider your family culture regarding food and body image. Is it helpful? Could some shifts be made to move away from shame, diet culture, or judgment?
- Consider not labeling foods as good or bad.
- Practice not judging or commenting on the size or shape of people's bodies.
- Read one of the books recommended for further study:

   Breaking Free from Body Shame by Jess Connolly;

   The Wisdom of Your Body by Dr. Hillary McBride;

   Intuitive Eating by Evelyn Tribole and Elyse Resch;

   How to Raise an Intuitive Eater by Sumner Brooks and Amee Severson; *Anti-Diet* by Christy Harrison; *Mothers, Daughters, and Body Image* by Dr. Hillary McBride.

- Learn more about media literacy and how to be a critical/mindful consumer of media.
- Explore a Health at Every Size approach.
- Reduce your time on social media.
- Unfollow social media accounts that don't build you up. Conversely, consider following accounts that demonstrate body diversity.
- After determining what such a practice would look like, engage in a daily or weekly prayer time that reminds you of God's tangible love for you.

- Talk with a friend or two about changing how you talk about food and your bodies.
- Plan a regular mindful walk, noticing beauty in your surroundings.
- Practice seeing true beauty in the world and in the people around you.

ACKNOWLEDGMENTS

Have you ever felt like something was laid on your heart? A certain message, dream, or next step? For me, the message of this book was like that on steroids. It burned within me and simply could not stay inside. I had to tell women what I've seen and learned.

Like most things in life, sharing this message takes a village. And I am beyond-words grateful for the people who have surrounded me with encouragement, patience, and the practical steps needed to get this message into the world. The book you now hold is a testament to miraculous connections, friends' and family's enduring support and patience, and what can only be explained as God's faithful working behind the scenes in profound and beautiful ways.

First, a huge thank-you to Jared for your patience when I had a "crazy" idea, your steadfast support in every form, and for believing in me always.

To Don Pape for tirelessly believing in me and this much-needed redefinition of beauty. Despite rejections and discouragement, you encouraged me to never give up. Thank you, thank you, thank you. You are a gifted agent and true friend.

To Jeff Braun at Bethany House Publishers for patiently standing by as this message unfolded and taking a chance on a new author. I am forever grateful to you, Jeff.

To Abbie Sprunger for seeing the heart of this message enough to connect me with Don so this could all happen. God has used you in my story in so many ways. Though we haven't been face-to-face many times, I consider you a dear friend.

To Allison Fallon for teaching me about the story arc and publishing and for helping give my message and story form in its earliest stages. Your work is invaluable and changes lives.

To my dad for planting the seed that I should write a book when it was the furthest thing from my mind.

To both my mom and dad for believing in me and being my forever cheerleaders, whatever I put my mind and heart to. For tuning in to, understanding, and championing the contours of my soul. For taking the time to listen intently to my stories, perspectives, and desires, and for doing and enjoying life together. For helping me know what it looks and feels like to be loved and known.

To Leanna for patiently reading my early drafts of blog posts, podcast intros, and book chapters. You are the Frasier to my Niles and my unofficial (unpaid) editor. You make me a better writer. Your practical help and steadfast belief in this message have been more meaningful and supportive than I can say.

To Emily for reminding me to lighten up when I get too serious and enjoy life, and for being a tireless advocate for my true self. Sometimes sisters are also your best friends.

To every podcast guest or interviewee from the original Mentor Series for taking the time to teach me about how you see beauty. Your lessons have changed me. I imagine they've changed many others too.

To all my friends who prayed for me, spoke words of truth or encouragement over me, and believed in me and this message being published when I doubted it. (Yes, that means you, Lance, for telling me you knew it was only a matter of time and it would happen. Thank you.)

To everyone who helped me in the journey detailed in this book. To the therapists and dietitians, I hope you know you save lives. Please keep up your amazing work. It makes a difference.

NOTES

Chapter One The Race to Nowhere

1. Shaun Dreisbach, "Shocking Body-Image News: 97% of Women Will Be Cruel to Their Bodies Today," *Glamour*, February 2, 2011, https://www.glamour.com/story/shocking-body-image-news-97-percent-of-women-will-be-cruel-to-their-bodies-today.

2. "Survey Finds Disordered Eating Behaviors Among Three Out of Four American Women," *Carolina Public Health Magazine*, September 26, 2008, https://sph.unc.edu/cphm/carolina-public-health-magazine-accelerate-fall-2008/survey-finds-disordered-eating-behaviors-among-three-out-of-four-american-women-fall-2008/.

3. "Busting the Myths About Eating Disorders," National Eating Disorders Association, https://www.nationaleatingdisorders.org/busting-myths-about-eating-disorders.

4. Edward Chesney, Guy M. Goodwin, and Seena Fazel, "Risks of All-Cause and Suicide Mortality in Mental Disorders: A Meta-Review," *World Psychiatry*, 68(7), (June 2014): 724–31.

Chapter Three Broken Beauty

1. Nichola Rumsey and Diana Harcourt, *The Oxford Handbook of the Psychology of Appearance* (Oxford: Oxford University Press, 2012), 175.

2. *The Illusionists* Press Kit: https://theillusionists.org/wp-content/uploads/2016/10/ILLUSIONISTS-presskit.pdf.

3. Ruth Striegel-Moore and Debra L. Franko, "Body Image Issues Among Girls and Women," in T. F. Cash and T. Pruzinsky, eds., *Body Image: A Handbook of Theory, Research, and Clinical Practice* (New York: Guilford Press, 2002), 183–191.

4. Jacinta Lowes and Marika Tiggemann, "Body Dissatisfaction, Dieting Awareness and the Impact of Parental Influence in Young Children," *The British Psychological Society*, 8 (2003): 135–147.

5. ANAD, "Eating Disorder Statistics," https://anad.org/eating-disorders-statistics/.

6. Glenn A. Gaesser, *Big Fat Lies: The Truth About Your Weight and Your Health* (Carlsbad, CA: Gurze Books, 2002), 28.

7. Jean Kilbourne, *Deadly Persuasion: Why Women and Girls Must Fight the Addictive Power of Advertising* (New York: Free Press, 1999), 74.

8. Kilbourne, *Deadly Persuasion*, 74.

9. Louise Story, "Anywhere the Eye Can See, It's Likely to See an Ad," *New York Times*, January 15, 2007, https://www.nytimes.com/2007/01/15/business/media/15everywhere.html.

10. Elena Rossini (2015). *The Illusionists* (film). Media Education Foundation.

11. *The Illusionists* Press Kit.

12. Jerry Suls and Ladd Wheeler, "Social Comparison Theory," in *Handbook of Theories of Social Psychology: Volume One*, eds. Paul A. M. Van Lange, Arie W. Kruglanski, and E. Tory Higgins (London: Sage Publications, 2012).

13. Emma Halliwell and Phillippa C. Diedrichs, "Influence of the Media" in *The Oxford Handbook of the Psychology of Appearance*, eds. Nichola Rumsey and Diana Harcourt (Oxford: Oxford University Press, 2012), 229.

14. *The Illusionists* Press Kit.

15. Helga Dittmar, Emma Halliwell, and Emma Striling, "Understanding the Impact of Thin Media Models on Women's Body-Focused Affect: The Roles of Thin-Ideal Internalization and Weight-Related Self-Discrepancy Activation in Experimental Exposure Effects," *Journal of Social and Clinical Psychology* 28(1) (January 2009): 44.

16. Eating disorders statistics, *National Association of Anorexia Nervosa and Associated Disorders*, retrieved February 7, 2014, from https://web.archive.org/web/20140502024231/http://www.anad.org/get-information/about-eating-disorders/eating-disorders-statistics/.

17. Jennifer L. Derenne and Eugene V. Beresin, "Body Image, Media, and Eating Disorders," *Academic Psychiatry* (May–June 2006), 257–61, https://link.springer.com/article/10.1176/appi.ap.30.3.257#citeas.

18. Morgan Fargo and Chloe Burcham, "'Slim Thick' Is Still a Trending Body Term, but What Actually Is It, and Is it Healthy?" *Women's Health*, May 26, 2022, https://www.womenshealthmag.com/uk/fitness/a35334392/slim-thick/.

19. Sarah E. McComb and Jennifer S. Mills, "The Effect of Physical Appearance Perfectionism and Social Comparison to Thin-, Slim-Thick, and Fit-Ideal Instagram Imagery on Young Women's Bodies," *Body Image, vol. 40* (March 2022): 165–175.

20. Sut Jhally, dir. *Killing Us Softly 4* (2010), film trailer featuring Jean Kilbourne, Media Education Foundation, https://www.youtube.com/watch?v=jWKXit_3rpQ.

21. Sut Jhally, dir. *Killing Us Softly 4*.

22. Stephanie Cooley, "The Filter Effect: People Distrust Websites Because of Manipulated Photos," *GlobeNewswire*, May 18, 2017, https://www.globenewswire.com/news-release/2017/05/18/1312618/0/en/The-Filter-Effect-People-Distrust-Websites-Because-of-Manipulated-Photos.html.

23. Unilever, "Behind the Selfie: Reversing the Damage of Digital Distortion," April 20, 2021, https://www.unilever.com/news/news-search/2021/behind-the-selfie-reversing-the-damage-of-digital-distortion/.

24. Derenne and Beresin, "Body Image, Media, and Eating Disorders."

25. Halliwell and Diedrichs, "Influence of the Media," 275.

26. Kilbourne, *Deadly Persuasion*, 132.

27. Lisa Mask and Celine M. Blanchard, "The Effects of 'Thin Ideal' Media on Women's Body Image Concerns and Eating-Related Intentions: The Beneficial Role of an Autonomous Regulation of Eating Behaviors," *Body Image* 8(4) (July 2011): 357–65.

28. Soledad Cruz-Saez, Aiziber Pascual, and Anna Wlodarczyk, "The Effect of Body Dissatisfaction on Disordered Eating: The Mediating Role of Self-Esteem and Negative Affect in Male and Female Adolescents," *Journal of Health Psychology* 25(8) (2020): 1098–1108.

29. Lifespan, "Negative Body Image Related to Depression, Anxiety and Suicidality," *ScienceDaily*, June 6, 2006, www.sciencedaily.com/releases/2006/06/060606224541.htm.

30. Sut Jhally, dir. *Killing Us Softly 4*.

31. Christy Harrison, *Anti-Diet: Reclaim Your Time, Money, Well-Being, and Happiness Through Intuitive Eating* (New York: Little, Brown Spark), 7.

32. Christine Osgood, (2022). *GES140 Introduction to Wellbeing* (11th ed.), Department of Wellbeing, Bethel University.

33. Harrison, *Anti-Diet*, 7.

34. Jane E. Brody, "Panel Criticizes Weight-Loss Programs," *New York Times*, April 2, 1992, https://www.nytimes.com/1992/04/02/us/panel-criticizes-weight-loss-programs.html; Alison Fildes, Judith Charlton, Caroline Rudisill, Peter Littlejohns, A Toby Prevost, and Martin C Guilford, "Probability of an Obese Person Attaining Normal Body Weight: Cohort Study Using Electronic Health Records," *American Journal of Public Health* 105(9) (September 2015): 54–59.

35. Harrison, *Anti-Diet*, 7.

36. "Orthorexia," *NEDA*, https://www.nationaleatingdisorders.org/learn/by-eating-disorder/other/orthorexia.

37. Oona Hanson, "Sending a Kid to College? Talk About Eating Disorders Before They Leave," *Your Teen for Parents*, https://yourteenmag.com/health/physical-health/eating-disorders-college.

38. Harrison, *Anti-Diet*, 6.

39. Laura Wood, "The U.S. Weight Loss Market 2022: Market Up 24% in 2021-ResearchAndMarkets.com," *Business Wire*, March 18, 2022, https://www.businesswire.com/news/home/20220318005208/en/The-U.S.-Weight-Loss-Market-2022-Market-Up-24-in-2021---ResearchAndMarkets.com.

40. Christine Michel Carter, "The Business of Feeding Health-Conscious Gen Z and Alpha Children," *Forbes*, October 2017, https://www.forbes.com/sites/christinecarter/2017/10/29/the-business-of-feeding-health-conscious-gen-z-and-alpha-children/?sh=1acbad7f6b28.

41. ABC News Staff "100 Million Dieters, $20 Billion: The Weight-Loss Industry by the Numbers," *ABC News*, May 2012, https://abcnews.go.com/Health/100-million-dieters-20-billion-weight-loss-industry/story?id=16297197.

42. "The Media's Unrealistic Idea of Beauty," *StudyMode Research*, https://www.studymode.com/essays/The-Medias-Unrealistic-Idea-Of-Beauty-543B836A5ED217BC.html.

43. Brené Brown, *Daring Greatly: How the Courage to Be Vulnerable Transforms the Way We Live, Love, Parent, and Lead* (New York: Gotham Books, 2012), 69.

44. Steve Moore, *Scripture of the Day*: September 22, 2016.

45. Sharlene Nagy Hesse-Biber, *Cult of Thinness, 2nd Edition* (Oxford: Oxford University Press, 2006), 156.

46. Sadie Lincoln (host), "Changing the Way You Feel about Your Body" with Dr. Hillary McBride (audio podcast), April 6, 2020. In *Present-Truth Conversations*, https://podcasts.apple.com/us/podcast/hillary-mcbride-changing-the-way-you-feel-about-your-body/id1506677715?i=1000470696785.

47. Lincoln, "Changing the Way You Feel About Your Body" with Dr. Hillary McBride.

48. Dictionary.com, s.v. "media literacy," https://dictionary.com/browse/media-literacy.

Chapter Four Slow Suicide

1. Dr. David Baker and Natacha Keramidas, "The Psychology of Hunger," *American Psychological Association*, vol. 44, no. 9 (October 2013), 6.

2. Arline Kaplan, "Anorexia and Brain Imaging," *Psychiatric Times*, vol. 27, issue 2 (February 5, 2010), www.psychiatrictimes.com/eating-disorders/anorexia-and-brain-imaging.

3. Kate Mulvey and Melissa Richards, *Decades of Beauty: The Changing Image of Women, 1890s to 1990s* (London: Hamlyn, 1998), 128.

4. Kilbourne, *Deadly Persuasion*, 130.

5. Helga Dittmar, "The Costs of Consumer Culture and the 'Cage Within': The Impact of the Material 'Good Life' and 'Body Perfect' Ideals on Individuals' Identity and Well-Being," *Psychological Inquiry*, vol. 18, no. 1 (2007), 23–31.

6. Kilbourne, *Deadly Persuasion*, 129.

7. Parker J. Palmer, *Let Your Life Speak: Listening for the Voice of Vocation* (San Francisco: Jossey-Bass, 2000), 11.

8. Palmer, *Let Your Life Speak*, 12.

Chapter Five The Villain

1. Curt Thompson, *The Soul of Shame: Retelling the Stories We Believe About Ourselves* (Downers Grove: IVP Books, 2015), 13.

2. Thompson, *The Soul of Shame*, 13.

3. Joe Connors and Anne Bradley, "Economic Freedom and the Path to Flourishing," Institute for Faith, Work, and Economics (2013), https://tifwe.org/wp-content/uploads/2013/10/Economic-Freedom-and-the-Path_Revised.pdf.

4. Connors and Bradley, "Economic Freedom and the Path to Flourishing."

5. Richard Rohr, *Falling Upward: A Spirituality for the Two Halves of Life* (San Francisco: Jossey-Boss, 2011), 93.

6. Richard Rohr, *Everything Belongs: The Gift of Contemplative Prayer* (New York: The Crossroad Publishing Company, 2003), 31.

7. Ephesians 6:12.

8. 1 Peter 5:8.

9. John 10:10.

10. Richard Linn Maisel, David Epston, and Ali Borden, *Biting the Hand That Starves You: Inspiring Resistance to Anorexia/Bulimia* (New York: W.W. Norton and Company, Inc., 2004), 52.

11. Maisel, Epston, and Borden, *Biting the Hand That Starves You*, 75.

12. Melissa Petruzzello, "Mammon: Biblical Literature," *Encyclopedia Britannica* (September 8, 2020), https://www.britannica.com/topic/mammon.

13. Petruzzello, "Mammon: Biblical Literature."

14. Greg Boyd, "Opting Out of the Mammon Game" (Sermon recording), April 3, 2022, https://whchurch.org/sermon/opting-out-of-the-mammon-game/.

15. Boyd, "Opting Out of the Mammon Game," April 3, 2022.

16. Brown, *Daring Greatly*, 69.

Chapter Six The Morality of Judgment

1. Rachel H. Salk and Renee Engeln-Maddox, "'If You're Fat, Then I'm Humongous!': Frequency, Content, and Impact of Fat Talk Among College Women," *Psychology of Women Quarterly*, vol. 35, issue 1 (March 2, 2011), 18–28.

2. Lincoln, "Changing the Way You Feel About Your Body" with Dr. Hillary McBride.

3. Thompson, *The Soul of Shame*, 28.

4. Thompson, *The Soul of Shame*, 29.

5. Christy Harrison, *Anti-Diet*, 25.

6. Harrison, *Anti-Diet*, 25.

7. Sabrina Strings, *Fearing the Black Body: The Racial Origins of Fat Phobia* (New York: New York University Press, 2019), 67.

8. Strings, *Fearing the Black Body*, 67.

9. Dianne Neumark-Sztainer, Mary Story, and Tanya Harris, "Beliefs and Attitudes About Obesity Among Teachers and School Health Care Providers Working with Adolescents," *Journal of Nutrition Education*, vol. 31, issue 1 (January 1999): 3–9.

10. Rebecca M. Puhl and Kelly M. King, "Weight Discrimination and Bullying," *Best Practice and Research Clinical Endocrinology and Metabolism* 27(2) (April 2013): 117–27.

11. Klea D. Bertakis and Rahman Azari, "The Impact of Obesity on Primary Care Visits," *Obesity Research* 13(9) (September 2005): 1615–23.

12. Regina Pingitore, Bernard Dugoni, et al., "Bias Against Overweight Job Applicants in a Simulated Employment Interview," *Journal of Applied Psychology* 79(6) (December 1994): 909–917.

13. Charles L. Baum and William L. Ford, "The Wage Effects of Obesity: A Longitudinal Study," *Health Economics* 13(9) (September 2004): 885–99.

14. Doris Bazzini, Lisa Curtin, et al., "Do Animated Disney Characters Portray and Promote the Beauty-Goodness Stereotype?" *Journal of Applied Social Psychology* 40(1) (2010): 2687–709.

15. Maisel, Epston, and Borden, *Biting the Hand That Starves You*, 24.

16. Rudolph M. Bell, *Holy Anorexia* (Chicago: University of Chicago Press, 1985).

17. Peter N. Stearns, *Fat History: Bodies and Beauty in the Modern West* (New York: New York University Press, 1997).

18. Harrison, *Anti-Diet*, 35.

19. Sindya N. Bhanoo, "Study Suggests BMI Scale Is Weighted Against African Americans," *Washington Post*, April 14, 2009, http://www.washingtonpost.com/wp -dyn/content/article/2009/04/13/AR2009041301823.html.

20. Katherine Flegel, Brian Kit, et al., "Association of All-Cause Mortality with Overweight and Obesity Using Standard Body Mass Index Categories: A Systematic Review and Meta-analysis," *JAMA* 309(1) (January 2, 2013): 71–82.

21. Harrison, *Anti-Diet*, 36.

22. Harrison, *Anti-Diet*, 44.

23. Harrison, *Anti-Diet*, 44.

24. J. Eric Oliver, *Fat Politics: The Real Story Behind America's Obesity Epidemic* (Oxford University Press, 2005), 30.

25. Harrison, *Anti-Diet*, 244.

26. Matthew 22:39.

27. Richard Rohr, *Everything Belongs*, 63.

Chapter Seven Human Again

1. Rohr, *Falling Upward*, xxii.

2. Rohr, *Falling Upward*, ix–x.

3. Rohr, *Falling Upward*, ix.

Chapter Eight The Body as a Miracle

1. Suzana Herculano-Houzel, "The Human Brain in Numbers: A Linearly Scaled-Up Primate Brain," *Frontiers in Human Neuroscience* (November 9, 2009), https://www.frontiersin.org/articles/10.3389/neuro.09.031.2009/full.

2. Rose Eveleth, "There Are 37.2 Trillion Cells in Your Body," *Smithsonian Magazine*, October 24, 2013, https://www.smithsonianmag.com/smart-news/there -are-372-trillion-cells-in-your-body-4941473/.

3. Genesis 2:7.

Chapter Nine Reimagining God

1. Psalm 139.

2. Zephaniah 3:17.

Chapter Ten Reversing the Baby Shower Effect

1. *American Psychological Association: APA Dictionary of Psychology*, s.v. "group polarization," https://dictionary.apa.org/group-polarization.

2. Curt Thompson, *The Soul of Shame: Retelling the Stories We Believe About Ourselves* (Downers Grove: IVP Books, 2015), 42.

3. Thompson, *The Soul of Shame*, 32.

Chapter Eleven A New Way to Define Beauty

1. C. S. Lewis, *The Weight of Glory* (New York: HarperCollins, 2001), 26.

2. Baxter Kruger, *The Great Dance: The Christian Vision Revisited* (Jackson, MS: Perichoresis, Inc., 2000).

3. Kristen Sheridan, dir. *August Rush*. 2007; [United States]: Warner Bros. Pictures, Odyssey Entertainment.

4. Lewis, *The Weight of Glory*, 45–46.

5. This suggestion comes from John Eldredge on episode 92 of the *Impossible Beauty* podcast.

Chapter Twelve Recovery as Resistance

1. Paul Hamburg, "The Media and Eating Disorders: Who Is Most Vulnerable?" Public Forum: Culture, Media and Eating Disorders (1998), Harvard Medical School.

2. Curt Thompson, *The Soul of Desire: Discovering the Neuroscience of Longing, Beauty, and Community* (Downers Grove, IL: InterVarsity Press, 2021, 45.

3. Thompson, *The Soul of Desire*, 69.

4. Christy Harrison, *Anti-Diet: Reclaim Your Time, Money, Well-Being, and Happiness Through Intuitive Eating* (New York: Little, Brown Spark, 2019), 33.

5. Rohr, *Falling Upward*, 97.

6. John 10:10.

7. Brown, *Daring Greatly*, 69.

A Three-Day Retreat Guide

1. Dictionary.com, s.v. "media literacy."

2. Brown, *Daring Greatly*, 69.

3. John 10:10.

4. Lincoln, "Changing the Way You Feel About Your Body" with Dr. Hillary McBride.

5. Lincoln, "Changing the Way You Feel About Your Body" with Dr. Hillary McBride.

6. Taken from Tara Owens, *Embracing the Body: Finding God in Our Flesh and Bone* (Downers Grove, IL: InterVaristy Press, 2015), 190–92. Copyright (c) 2015 by Tara M. Owens. Used by permission of InterVarsity Press, P.O. Box 1400, Downers Grove, IL 60515, USA. www.ivpress.com.

7. Question taken from John Eldredge on episode 92 of the *Impossible Beauty* podcast.

8. John 10:10.

9. Owens, *Embracing the Body*, 18–19.

10. Owens, *Embracing the Body*, 18–19.

ABOUT THE AUTHOR

Melissa Louise Johnson, MA, LMFT, is a marriage and family therapist and a certified spiritual director. She holds two master's degrees—in marriage and family therapy and in spiritual formation—and teaches a course on soul well-being at Bethel University in St. Paul, Minnesota. She believes we're most fully alive when we're able to connect deeply with God, others, and ourselves.

She is also the founder of *Impossible Beauty*, a blog and podcast dedicated to redefining beauty as "the Life of God at work in us and among us" (impossible-beauty.com). Her writing and podcast interviews seek to uncover what true beauty is, what it is not, and how we go about finding beauty in a broken world.

Melissa lives with her husband, Jared, near Minneapolis, Minnesota.